The
BUSY CHRISTIAN'S
GUIDE to BUSYNESS

The

BUSY CHRISTIAN'S GUIDE to BUSYNESS

Tim Chester

Inter-Varsity Press
Norton Street, Nottingham NG7 3HR, England

Email: ivp@ivpbooks.com
Website: www.ivpbooks.com

First published 2006
Reprinted 2007
New edition 2008
Reprinted 2009, 2010

British Library Cataloguing-in-Publication Data
A catalogue record for this book is available from the British Library.

ISBN: 978-1-84474-302-5

Set in Monotype Dante 12/15pt

Typeset in Great Britain by Servis Filmsetting Ltd, Stockport, Cheshire
Printed and bound in Great Britain by Ashford Colour Press, Gosport,
Hampshire

*Inter-Varsity Press publishes Christian books that are true to the Bible and that communicate
the gospel, develop discipleship and strengthen the church for its mission in the world.*

*Inter-Varsity Press is closely linked with the Universities and Colleges Christian Fellowship,
a student movement connecting Christian Unions in universities and colleges throughout
Great Britain, and a member movement of the International Fellowship of Evangelical
Students. Website: www.uccf.org.uk*

CONTENTS

START HERE

Our Christian lives can be full of good intentions to do more for God, but time and again those good intentions are sapped by the pace of our lives. Sermons, conferences, talks, books all urge us to spend more time praying, studying the Bible, sharing the gospel, building community, caring for the needy, campaigning for justice – and on it goes. But most Christians feel their lives are already over-full. Some Christians, because of ill-health or unemployment, struggle with the opposite problem. They wish they had more to do. But everywhere you look in the church today there are busy Christians.

These comments are from members of my church. See how many you sympathize with.

- How can I balance time between work, friends and church?
- I know too many people – I don't have the time to keep up with them all.
- Is busyness bad?
- Why do Christians seem busier than non-Christians?
- I feel trapped in my lifestyle.
- Who's in charge of my time?
- I always seem to take on too much.

- Please clear my diary!
- I feel guilty about the tensions between work, church and family.
- I just don't want to be busy all the time.

There are many challenges facing the church today. But alongside all of them is this problem of time and busyness. Whatever new ideas we come up with for church or mission, we need to find the time to do them! In his book *The Tyranny of Time*, Robert Banks (1983) says: 'Our attitude to time is not an extra commitment or idea. It is the medium in which everything else is done. It affects everything.' There's so much we want to do; so many issues; so many opportunities. But so little time. We could argue about what the most crucial concerns are facing Christians today. But unless we sort out a Christian view of busyness, we might not find time to debate them, let alone do anything.

This book won't give you an extra hour in your day or an extra day in your week. But it will help you think through why you feel so busy and what you might do about it. It will show how faith in God can make a real difference to the way we live in a high-pressure world. When people talk about their busyness it can be like watching someone's home movie. You get a version of their life, but they're never in the picture. The reality is that our behaviour is driven by our beliefs. If you're serious about tackling your busy behaviour you'll have to put your own heart in the picture. You'll have to face up to the deceptions you live by and make choices to replace them with the truth.

Each chapter is designed so it can be read while you're commuting to work – unless you drive to work, in which case you should petition the publishers for an audio version!

1. SLOW DOWN, I WANT TO GET OFF!

Have you ever been irritated because your train left ten minutes late? Or because there was a queue at the supermarket till? Or because people in front of you were dawdling or driving slowly? Or even because someone took their time to get to the point? Then according to cardiologist Meyer Friedman (1999) you suffer from 'hurry sickness'. The funny thing about hurry sickness is that sufferers often think they're okay while those who are immune are portrayed as being sick.

1. Do you regularly work thirty minutes a day longer than your contracted hours?
2. Do you check work emails and phone messages at home?
3. Has anyone ever said to you: 'I didn't want to trouble you because I know how busy you are'?
4. Do your family or friends complain about not getting time with you?

5. If tomorrow evening was unexpectedly freed up, would you use it to work or do a household chore?
6. Do you often feel tired during the day or do you find your neck and shoulders aching?
7. Do you often exceed the speed limit while driving?
8. Do you make use of any flexible working arrangements offered by your employers?
9. Do you pray with your children regularly?
10. Do you have enough time to pray?
11. Do you have a hobby in which you are actively involved?
12. Do you eat together as a family or household at least once a day?

If you mainly answered 'yes' to questions 1–7 and 'no' to questions 8–12 then maybe you have a busyness problem.

Busy at work

The average British worker puts in an 8.7-hour day. If you enter the office at 8.30am and take an hour for lunch that means you leave at 6.12pm. The average German or Italian worker leaves one hour before you. They're already at home enjoying a lager or glass of Chianti. That's if your continental counterpart actually went to work. While UK workers get 28 days holiday a year including bank holidays, French workers get 47 days, Germans 41 days, Spaniards 46 days and Italians 44 days. Brits do, however, work less than the Americans, who work a 47-hour week – longer now than in the 1920s.

Contracted working hours have in fact changed little in the last fifty years, but they don't reflect the hours people actually do. The average British worker does the equivalent of eight weeks unpaid overtime each year. It's as if you worked each January and February without pay. Three-quarters of managers feel working late or at weekends is the only way to deal with the workload. It's not just office workers. Machine operators and supermarket checkout staff commonly work five extra hours a week. Less than half of all workers use their full holiday entitlement, while the average lunch 'hour' actually lasts 27 minutes. Plus it takes an average of 38 minutes to get to work. UK managers have the longest commute in Europe – 53 minutes. And none of these statistics takes into account the time spent thinking about work issues while you're sitting in the bath or dining with your family.

No wonder over a third of people agree that 'in the evenings I am so tired I just fall asleep on the sofa' (Jones, 2003). Moreover, the pensions crisis suggests most of us will be on this treadmill until we're 70. 'One of the greatest challenges facing Christians in the UK', says Mark Greene (2004) of the London Institute for Contemporary Christianity, 'is to live the abundant life of Christ in the face of the dehumanizing, relationally destructive and emotionally, physically and spiritually debilitating effects of the contemporary work-place.'

Busy at play

Even our time off can be hard work. Our secular age tends to give material answers to spiritual problems. So leisure has become a thing you 'do' or 'buy'. We 'relax' by going to the gym, driving across town to a late night movie or spending an afternoon shopping – and nothing is more tiring than shopping! We no longer 'stroll' or 'ramble'; now we 'hike' with walking poles to propel us along. Leisure is no longer rest; leisure is consumption. And

Even our time off can be hard work. Our secular age tends to give material answers to spiritual problems.

so we must work hard to afford our new leisure lifestyles! As Ellen Goodman (2004) comments: 'Normal is getting dressed in clothes that you buy for work, driving through traffic in a car that you are still paying for, in order to get to the job you need so you can pay for the clothes, the car, and the house that you leave empty all day in order to afford to live in it.' Labour saving devices have increased, but we also have larger homes and more possessions that need more maintenance.

'The problem with television is that people must sit and keep their eyes glued to a screen; the average American family hasn't time for it.' So said the *New York Times* in 1939 (Ward, 2003). Looking back it seems a crazy statement. But is it? Maybe it was true then and maybe it's true now. We have enough to do without watching television, and yet watch television we do for hours on end. And then we wonder why the rest of life seems so busy.

Too busy to be healthy

More than eight out of ten British workers feel their health has been harmed by work demands. One in five men has visited the doctor with work-related stress. Sixty percent of us feel our workloads are sometimes out of control. One in five feels this way most of the time. For many, a nervous breakdown is the only way out. One church leader told me: 'I sometimes long to be hospitalized – nothing too painful, but I'd have no responsibilities and lots of attention.'

'We'd like to be unhappy,' sang Bing Crosby, 'but we never do have the time.' Once upon a time people 'convalesced' after illness. 'Time will heal,' we said. Not any more. Adverts for cold remedies used to portray a patient tucked up in bed sipping a hot drink. Now they show people turning up unexpectedly at work, high on medicine to beat off the competition. You don't even have to stop to take your medicine.

'We even have products which dissolve on the tongue,' they boast, 'so you can take them on the go!' In the seventeenth century Samuel Pepys had a 40-day recovery period after a kidney stone operation. Today three-quarters of us go to work when we're ill, even though a ten-year study by University College London showed that workers who don't take time off when ill have double the rate of heart disease.

With so much going on in our lives, where can we steal some extra time from? These days eight or nine hours sleep seems positively feckless. And so on average we sleep one hour less than we need each night. Although the need for sleep can vary from six to ten hours between different individuals, adults require on average eight hours. In fact the average night's sleep is 7.04 hours. That's down two hours from the 1910 average! No wonder we're all so tired.

Too busy to think

'I get the impression that the biggest sacrifice for people engaging with anything is that they just don't have the time and space to think about it!' Jill works for a Christian anti-poverty campaign. She told me: 'Plenty of people want quick actions, but the actual work of taking *time to think* seems unmanageable. People's minds are full and the "no more room" light is flashing!'

'Time will tell,' people used to say, but today we can't wait that long. We confuse information and wisdom. Access to data does not make you wise. Wisdom takes study and reflection. Indeed true wisdom is found through a relationship with God. *'The fear of the LORD is the beginning of knowledge'* (Proverbs 1:7). But this wisdom does not become out of date with the next bulletin. *'All men are like grass, and all their glory is like the flowers of the field . . . The grass withers and the flowers fall, but the word of our God stands for ever'* (Isaiah 40:6, 8).

Too busy for relationships

In Bill Forsyth's film *Local Hero* (1983) Mac MacIntyre is an American oil executive sent to the Scottish village of Ferness to negotiate the building of an oil refinery. At first he is puzzled by the eccentricities of the inhabitants, but as the film progresses he is charmed by this community whose slow pace of life has weathered the centuries. Although somewhat romantic, the charm works on the viewer as well. Films of small, rural communities – films like *Local Hero*, *Waking Ned* and *Amazing Grace* – appeal to us because they portray the slower, more relational way of life for which we yearn. We want to live in the Shire rather than in *Lord of the Rings'* Isengard. One survey found that 72% of managers had been criticized by family and friends for spending too much time working.

We are 'bowling alone', as Harvard Professor Robert Putnam puts it (Putnam, 2000). There used to be bowling leagues across the United States. But, he observes, people no longer commit to clubs and societies. They still go bowling, either alone or in 'informal groups' – we don't have time for a regular activity. And what is true for sports clubs is true for social involvement. Seventy-two percent of managers claim overwork has restricted their ability to get involved in community affairs. Graduate women used to combine homemaking with community work; now they're in the workplace. Plus 'flexible' working means your free time may not coincide with mine so it's hard for us to work together on a local project.

Paul Tripp describes a married couple whom everyone thought were stalwarts of the local church. Then one day Paul got a call from the husband asking for an urgent meeting. It turned out they had been physically fighting for years. How was it, Paul asks, that this had been happening without any one in the church knowing? He concludes:

Perhaps the simplest reason for our lack of self-disclosing candour is that no one asks. The typical rhythms of our lives militate against going below the surface. In the busyness of life it seems intrusive to ask questions that cannot be answered without self-disclosure. Yet there is a way in which we all hunger for relationships of that quality. These are the relationships in which the Redeemer does his good work (Tripp, 2002).

Too busy for Jesus

Christians are susceptible to all the time pressures other people experience, but we add a few of our own. We make a virtue of hard work. We place a high premium on family time. And then we add in Christian meetings and responsibilities in church. As a result, suggests Robert Banks, 'with respect to time, Christians are a good deal worse off than many' (Banks, 1983). A friend told me his church had identified 'time impoverishment' as one of the major challenges it faces. Does your daily prayer time ever feel hurried? Do you even have a daily prayer time? Does church involvement ever feel like another unwelcome demand? In 2004 artist Michael Gough created an exhibition entitled 'Iconography'. An actor dressed as an archetypal Jesus posed around London, blessing passers-by, while Gough discreetly photographed the results. 'No-one engages him in conversation,' Gough comments. 'People in the City have appointments to honour, meetings to attend, deals to make, lunch to buy.' We are too busy for Jesus.

Who hit the accelerator?

What's the first thing you do when you wake in the morning? Chances are you check the time. In medieval times people lived by the sun and the seasons. But the factories of industrial revolution required a coordinated workforce. 'The clock, not the steam engine,' claims Lewis Mumford, 'is the key

machine of the industrial age' (cited in Banks, 1983). The first
factory floors were dominated by large clocks and workers
were conditioned to accept clock time through a system of
fines. Plus the new light bulbs turned night into day. Henry
Ford realized he could run three eight-hour shifts every day
instead of one nine-hour shift. Tonight seven million people
in the UK are working. Historian Eric Hobsbawn (1969) comments: 'Industry brings the tyranny of the clock . . . the
measurement of life not in seasons or even weeks and days,
but in minutes, and above all a mechanized *regularity* of work
which conflicts not only with tradition, but with all the incli-
nations of a humanity as yet unconditioned into it.' Today we
live life under the shadow of the clock. Children are conditioned to live by 'periods' at school. Church life, too, is
affected. We don't take as long as it takes; instead meetings
run to schedule. British Christians sometimes laugh at
African churches where everyone arrives late and meetings
can run on for hours. But that we find such habits strange
reveals the extent to which we have become slaves to the
clock.

The table opposite summarizes how patterns of work and
rest have changed. You would be unwise to complain too
loudly about your working hours in front of your Victorian
ancestors. Today we work fewer hours than nineteenth-
century factory workers and domestic servants. The 1847 Ten
Hours Act limited the working week in the textile industry to
60 hours – still a lot more than the contracted hours of most
people today.

But the nature of work has changed. People speak of 'work
intensification'. Jobs in our information age typically involve
complex tasks and lots of autonomy. Such high discretion jobs
create more opportunities for self-fulfilment, but also more
opportunities for stress. A hundred years ago people went

Changing patterns of work and rest

Pre-Industrial Life	Industrial Life	Post-Industrial Life
the workplace is in the home	the workplace is separate from home	the boundaries between work and home are blurred
the whole family is involved in domestic and commercial activity	men go out to work while women work in the home	men and women are in the workplace, but women do most of the domestic chores
work and home in the same location	walk to work	a long commute to work
seasonal fluctuations in workload plus many holy days	long working hours and no holidays	constant pressure at work with two to four weeks' holiday
people working enough to maintain their standard of living	people working enough to maintain their standard of living	people working to attain an ever higher standard of living
high autonomy	low autonomy	high autonomy
specialized manual skills	one or two skills honed by years of practice	constantly needing to update skills and knowledge
a slow pace of life	a slow pace of life outside of work	a fast pace of life in both work and leisure
regulated by daylight and seasons	regulated by the clock	self-regulated
dividing time into days	dividing time into hours	dividing time into minutes
work itself is seen as fulfilling	work itself is seen as fulfilling	aspiring to jobs that are intrinsically fulfilling

home physically tired. No trip to the gym. Now most of us go home mentally worn out. We go to the gym to work out the frustrations of the day. A hundred years ago blue collar workers worked longer hours than white collar workers; now it's the other way round. When people say we are busier than ever, 'we' means 'we the middle-classes'. It could be that the issue of busyness has 'our' attention because it's now a middle-class phenomenon.

In pre-industrial times families lived, worked and played together. The exhortation to 'make time' for family would have been meaningless. But with the industrial revolution men went out to work while women worked at home. In post-industrial societies women have again entered the work-place – 70% of them. The result is that many women find themselves working a 'double shift': out at work during the day, household chores at night. In the information age, work is intruding into leisure time. Sixty percent of us read work emails at home or on holiday. Government figures suggest that working parents spend twice as long dealing with emails as playing with their children (Honoré, 2004).

Faster and faster

Previous generations measured their lives with diaries. Today we apportion our lives with minutes. Letters were dated, now emails are clocked to the second. In our mobile phone culture people expect to be able to talk to us at any time, anywhere. Richard Powers (2004) talks about 'the contagion of real time': 'In real time, every second counts. Every minute must be max-imized. Since we cannot stop the escaping moments, we have our machines give us the next best thing: two moments, crammed into one. Split screen. Multitasking. Mobile wireless voicemail message forwarding. RSS feeds. Picture-in-a-picture. We don't need to miss a thing. In fact, we can't . . . In real time,

we live in two minds, three tenses, and four continents at once
. . . In short we have grown so good at mastering time that
nanoseconds now weigh heavy on our hands.' The number of
people who 'always feel rushed' jumped 50% between the
1960s and 1990s (Putnam, 2000).

Consider someone whose job requires them to know about
a subject. You might be a doctor keeping up to date with medical
advances; a salesperson expected to know your market; a
teacher expected to know the latest government advice; a
church leader expected to know – well, almost everything.
Today there is an almost inexhaustible range of information
sources for you to keep up with: television, books, journals,
websites, networks, newspapers and 100,000 Google hits. You
can never be sure you've covered everything. And it's constantly
changing. We have 24 hours of rolling news, RSS feeds, email
bulletins. Everything you read is soon out of date. In the past
people could be polymaths – experts in more than one subject.
Today most people are busy struggling to remain up to date in
one subject. Four out of every five managers give 'the quantity
of information' as one reason for long hours.

When I first worked in an office we had a tea lady who
came round each morning and afternoon. It was the last ves-
tige of a great British tradition whose demise we must now
lament – the tea break. The word 'elevenses' is slipping out of
our vocabulary. What makes tea such a great drink is that it
can neither be brewed nor drunk quickly. The tea leaves
should be allowed to infuse (the very word makes you slow
down) in a teapot. But now we mash the bag in the cup to save
time. We sip café lattes at our desks out of disposable cups.
We are offered non-spill lids so we can drink while we walk.
A Mexican friend once expressed to me in no uncertain terms
his horror at English people who eat their lunch 'on the run'.
We don't so much take a lunch break as 'refuel'.

Somewhere over the rainbow

I used to think my busyness problem was temporary. I was busy just at that moment, but it wouldn't last. Somewhere over the rainbow life would slow down. This month was busy, but next month looked better and my diary for the month after was almost empty. But of course a couple of months down the line my diary had filled up like every other month. Things don't change of their own accord. Working a bit harder to get ahead doesn't work either. There are other pressures going on that fill time as soon as we create it – like dry sand falling back into a hole while we frantically dig faster. The fact is, if you want to tackle your busyness, you will need to make deliberate choices.

2. IS BUSY BAD?

Work was despised in Greek and Roman society. Aristotle said it was 'devoid of nobility and hostile to perfection of character' (Ryken, 1989). Manual labour was for slaves. The élite were left to pursue the mental activities of art, politics and philosophy. The Romans were more industrious, but their achievements were built on the back of slave labour. Both cultures showed little respect to those on whose labour they depended. A freeman who worked blurred the distinction between slave and free, and that risked subverting the social order.

Greek and Roman attitudes continued in the medieval church. Work was perceived as punishment for sin, with no intrinsic value. Some monastic orders said work was important, but this was religious and intellectual work like copying manuscripts. Menial tasks were left to lay brothers. Other orders commended work as a means to humility, but it humbled only because it was demeaning. Thomas Aquinas, the great medieval Catholic theologian, developed a hierarchy of professions with the contemplative life firmly at the top.

Attitudes were transformed by the Protestant Reformation. 'What seem to be secular works,' said Martin Luther, 'are actually the praise of God and represent an obedience which is well pleasing to him' (McGrath, 1991). Housework might have 'no obvious appearance of holiness, yet those very household chores are more to be valued than all the works of monks and nuns'. You didn't need to leave the world for a monastery to serve God. You could glorify God in the ordinary. 'Our Saviour Christ,' said the English Reformer Hugh Latimer, 'was a carpenter, and got his living with great labour. Therefore let no man disdain to follow him in a common calling and occupation. For as he blessed our nature with taking upon him the shape of man, so in his doing he blessed all occupations and arts' (McGrath, 1991). The Puritan William Perkins said: 'The action of a shepherd in keeping sheep is as good a work before God as a minister preaching' (Ryken, 1989). Work is now tainted by sin, but work came before the fall. Humanity was made to share God's purposes in creation through work. And so hard work became an ideal in Protestant countries.

The very first settlers of America hoped to find an idyll of such abundance that they could recreate an idealized Greece and Rome in which free men lived a life of leisure. But the second wave of settlers, the Pilgrim Fathers with their Reformation work ethic, had no such delusions. They came to tame the wilderness, proving themselves the true people of God. When Europeans visited the New World a generation later they were amazed by the industrious pace of life and disappointed at the lack of leisure opportunities. But it was not yet a society dedicated to work. Work was seasonal and the

Sabbath was honoured. The industrial revolution was to change all that.

The industrial revolution brought what William Blake called the 'dark Satanic mills' and with them a new morality to justify their long working hours and poor conditions. Whereas the Greeks and Romans had made leisure without work their ideal, this ethic was all work and no play. Thomas Carlyle claimed in the nineteenth century: 'Man was created to work, not to speculate, or feel, or dream . . . Every idle moment is treason' (Hodgkinson, 2004).

> There is a perennial nobleness, and even sacredness, in Work . . . The latest Gospel in this world is, Know thy work and do it . . . If this is not 'worship,' then I say, the more pity for worship; for this is the noblest thing yet discovered under God's sky. Who are thou that complainest of thy life of toil? Complain not. Look up, my wearied brother; see the fellow Workman there, in God's Eternity . . . sacred Band of the Immortals, celestial Bodyguard of the Empire of Mankind (Thomas, 1999).

Work, according to Carlyle, is the new gospel offering salvation and immortality. Professor Geoffrey Best (1979) comments, 'Work, it is not too much to say, was a cult for the respectable classes. Carlyle never wasted breath less fruitfully than in recommending them to give themselves to work. They had it in their bones and they made sure that their employees got it in theirs.' In *Self-Help* (1859), which sold over 250,000 copies, Samuel Smiles said: 'National progress is the sum of individual industry, energy, and uprightness, as national decay is of individual idleness, selfishness, and vice' (Golby, 1986). Charles Dickens parodied this attitude in *Little Dorrit* (1857). The clerk and rent-collector Pancks says:

What else do you suppose I think I am made for? Nothing. Rattle me out of bed early, set me going, give me as short a time as you like to bolt my meals in, and keep me at it. Keep me always at it, and I'll keep you always at it, you keep somebody else always at it. There you are with the Whole Duty of Man in the commercial country.

'The Whole Duty of Man' is a reference to a popular book of Christian morality from the seventeenth century the title of which was taken from Ecclesiastes 12:13: *'Fear God and keep his commandments, for this is the whole duty of man.'* This, suggests Dickens, has been replaced by a new duty – the duty of commercial activity.

Between 1732 and 1758 Benjamin Franklin, one of the founding fathers of modern America, published *Poor Richard's Almanack.* Widely read at the time, it contained numerous maxims in which Franklin extols a philosophy of hard work and thrift, many of which have found their way into common usage:

- God helps them that help themselves.
- Early to bed and early to rise, makes a man healthy, wealthy, and wise.
- Never leave that till tomorrow which you can do today.
- There are no gains without pains.
- Plough deep while sluggards sleep and you shall have corn to sell and to keep.
- Trouble springs from idleness and grievous toil from needless ease.
- A sleeping fox catches no poultry.

Christians often joined this moral crusade for hard work. In the sixth century Pope Gregory the Great listed the so-called 'seven deadly sins' as pride, envy, anger, avarice, sadness, gluttony and lust. Other versions listed 'acedia' (or 'accidie') which meant spiritual apathy – the opposite of zeal for God. Over time, however, this become sloth – the opposite of hard work. The sin of sadness was replaced by the sin of idleness. It was presumably now okay to be miserable and moan as long as you were busy!

The work-centred ethic:
work is good and leisure is bad

Two contrasting views of work and leisure are evident. One is what we might call 'the work-centred ethic': work is good and leisure is bad or work is central and leisure is peripheral. We are to welcome work as a moral good; as something which is improving. Our culture has made busyness a virtue. The nineteenth-century moralists have been replaced by today's management gurus. They promote a life of self-fulfilment through high activity and continuous improvement.

The leisure-centred ethic:
leisure is good and work is bad

The second view is 'the leisure-centred ethic'. The Greeks and Romans aspired to a life of leisure free from work. This ethic is making something of a comeback in reaction to our contemporary workaholic culture. Recent book titles bear witness to this: *How to be Idle*, *The Importance of Being Lazy*, *The Joy of Laziness* and *The Play Ethic*.

But both ethics are exploitative. The work ethic is the ideology of capitalism, designed to create diligent workers and consumers in the interest of good business. It not only justifies overwork, it makes it a moral good! As Bertrand Russell said: 'The rich preach the dignity of labour, while taking care themselves to remain undignified in this respect' (Russell,

1932). (Russell argued for a four-hour working day.) Christian writer Tony Payne (2001) says: 'Clock-time is a very modern concept, and has more to do with the demands of industry than the demands of godliness.'

But the idyllic life of leisure advocated in the leisure ethic is equally exploitative. It's really possible only at the expense of other people's servitude. Greek and Roman leisure was built on the backs of slaves. And the new leisure ethic feeds off other people's work in the same way. It may be the hippy living off state benefits; the upper-class idler living off inherited wealth; the employee throwing a sickie; or the downsizer who has made enough to escape to the country pad. It sounds very romantic, but in truth it's bourgeois. Tom Hodgkinson (2004) admits as much: 'The real treat,' he says, 'is to be derived from not working *while others toil*.' More of our leisure is at the expense of other people's exploited hard work than we realize. If I save money for a night out because I buy cheap, imported goods then the price of my leisure is paid by sweat shop workers overseas. Even when such links are not apparent, we can't live a life of leisure while others are poor. The sin of Sodom, according to Ezekiel, was that '*She and her daughters were arrogant, overfed and unconcerned; they did not help the poor and needy*' (Ezekiel 16:49). Even if we no longer need a salary we are to go on serving other people.

The Bible commends hard work
'A Mars a day helps you work, rest and play' the advertising jingle used to go. I'm not sure about the beneficial effects of chocolate, but the pattern of work, rest and play is a biblical one. We are invited to consider the ant:

> *Go to the ant, you sluggard; consider its ways and be wise! It has no*
> *commander, no overseer or ruler, yet it stores its provisions in summer*

and gathers its food at harvest. How long will you lie there, you
sluggard? When will you get up from your sleep? A little sleep, a little
slumber, a little folding of the hands to rest – and poverty will come on
you like a bandit and scarcity like an armed man (Proverbs 6:6–11).

A little sleep, a little slumber, a few more minutes in bed,
an evening on the sofa with the remote control. Consider the
ant and learn the merits of hard work. Notice, too, that the
ant acts ahead of time. It stores food in summer in preparation for the winter. Some people use their time poorly for
want of foresight and planning. We should plan to use our
time well.

In the parable of the talents (Matthew 25:14–30) the servants of the king are judged according to their use of time in
his service. The men who put their *'money to work'* are commended. But the third is judged as a *'wicked, lazy servant'*
(verse 26). Our great aim in life should be to hear the words:
'Well done, good and faithful servant' (verse 23). Earlier generations of Christians had a strong sense of needing to give an
account before God for their use of time. Robert Murray
M'Cheyne (1966) wrote in his journal: 'What right have I to
steal and abuse my Master's time?' A few weeks later he
wrote: 'Not a trait worth remembering! And yet these four-
and-twenty hours must be accounted for.'

Paul also commends hard work. *'Make it your ambition,'* he
tells the Thessalonians, *'to lead a quiet life, to mind your own busi-*
ness and to work with your hands, just as we told you, so that your
daily life may win the respect of outsiders and so that you will not be
dependent on anybody' (1 Thessalonians 4:11–12). This 'ambition'
is a long way from the ambitions of today's career-minded
workers. The goal is a *'quiet life'* that commends the gospel, not
a high-flying life in the limelight. In 2 Thessalonians 3:6 Paul
says Christians are *'to keep away from every brother who is idle'*.

He points to his own example. *'We were not idle when we were with you, nor did we eat anyone's food without paying for it. On the contrary, we worked night and day, labouring and toiling so that we would not be a burden to any of you'* (verses 7–8). He worked in this way *'to make ourselves a model for you to follow'* (verse 9). Paul and his companions worked *'night and day in order not to be a burden to anyone'* (1 Thessalonians 2:9). Presumably this involved Paul making tents by day and teaching the gospel in the evening. It is perhaps a model more church leaders should follow. We assume freedom from secular work is the ideal for ministers, but Paul didn't. It was important for him to set an example to new Christians of earning one's way.

Paul's rule is: *'If a man will not work, he shall not eat'* (2 Thessalonians 3:10). *'We hear that some among you are idle. They are not busy; they are busybodies. Such people we command and urge in the Lord Jesus Christ to settle down and earn the bread they eat'* (verses 11–12). Paul's condemnation of idlers is strong. The church should provide for those genuinely in need, such as the elderly widows. But Paul warns Timothy not to provide financial support to young widows (1 Timothy 5). The church shouldn't support people who can support themselves. Paul isn't saying we must fill every moment with activity. You don't need to feel guilty whenever you sit down for a cup of tea. He's saying that love requires that we provide for ourselves and others in need (Ephesians 4:28). To live off the hard work of others is selfishness. This condemnation of idleness is all the more striking given that in Greek and Roman society idleness was virtuous and noble. Paul was being truly counter-cultural. He's condemning the idle rich rather than the unemployed poor.

The Bible commends rest

The climax of creation is the Sabbath-rest of God (Genesis 2:1–3). God didn't rest because he was tired. He rested because the job was done. God is still at work in the world – sustaining creation and bringing about our salvation (John 5:17). But *'the heavens and the earth were completed'*. The fourth commandment recalls this Sabbath-rest of God. *'Remember the Sabbath day by keeping it holy,'* the people of Israel were told. *'Six days you shall labour and do all your work, but the seventh day is a Sabbath to the LORD your God.'* The reason for the Sabbath is this: *'For in six days the LORD made the heavens and the earth, the sea, and all that is in them, but he rested on the seventh day'* (Exodus 20:8–11). Rest is godly because rest is God-like. We rest because God himself rested.

The reason given for the Sabbath in Deuteronomy 5 is slightly different. *'Remember that you were slaves in Egypt and that the LORD your God brought you out of there with a mighty hand and an outstretched arm. Therefore the LORD your God has commanded you to observe the Sabbath day'* (Deuteronomy 5:15). The Sabbath here is based on the Israelites' own experience of redemption from slavery. The word 'labour' in verse 13 (*'Six days you shall labour'*) is the same as 'slave' in verse 15. The Sabbath was a symbol of salvation from slavery under Pharaoh's reign to blessing under God's reign. The goal of creation is the same as the goal of redemption: that God's people might share God's reign of rest and blessing. The law ensured that God's reign was experienced as blessing by all people. It prohibited work without rest – the experience of slaves. Unlike the inherent exploitation of the work-centred and leisure-centred ethics, the biblical pattern of work and rest is liberating. Rich and poor alike are to work six days; rich and poor alike are to enjoy rest.

The Sabbath day played a distinctive role in the Mosaic covenant. It was a sign of the covenant just as circumcision was a sign in the Abrahamic covenant (Exodus 31:12–17). It was a marker of the distinctiveness of the Jewish people in God's purposes. Now, however, the identity of God's people is found in Christ (Ephesians 2:11–18; Colossians 2:16–17). The Sabbath day was a pointer to the coming reign of rest that Jesus offers us. We are no longer under the letter of the Mosaic law (Romans 7:6; 1 Corinthians 9:20–21; Hebrews 8:13). The Sabbath day pointed to the rest we now enjoy in the gospel, which we will explore in chapters 6–12.

The challenge of work–life balance may not be as complicated as we sometimes imagine.

But the Sabbath pattern may still offer a good guide. The challenge of work–life balance may not be as complicated as we sometimes imagine. We don't have to be legalistic about Sabbath observance, but why not do your work and chores in six days and spend one day resting? Why not set aside a day for rest and play, free from work, consumption and maybe even some forms of technology? Why not at least ensure your week includes all the rest you need? The evidence suggests people who rest regularly are more productive – though the goal of Sabbath is not increased productivity, but the glory of God. What constitutes work and rest will vary from person to person. Some people find gardening a chore; others finding it relaxing. You'll know which activities you find restful.

Binge resting

Recently a brochure dropped out of a Christian magazine. On the front were four pictures. The first showed a mother in the rain, weighed down with shopping bags, trying to control two grumpy children. The second showed a family slumped on the sofa, obviously bored, watching the television. The third showed a business man at a desk overflowing with paperwork, talking on the phone, clearly stressed and overworked, with a look of despair on his face. The fourth showed a woman in a church with cleaning equipment looking at the rotas on the notice board. On each rota was the word 'you'. At the bottom were the words: 'Looks familiar? The answer may be closer than you think . . .' Here, it seemed, was the answer to busyness and overwork. Inside was the offer of a Christian holiday. The answer, it turns out, was 'Give yourself a break!' In fact the answer was to give yourself an expensive holiday in France. This was clearly only an answer for wealthy people.

I was disappointed because this buys into our culture's assumption that holidays are the answer to busyness. Holidays are a great opportunity to keep in touch with people, enjoy God's creation and experience different cultures. But holidays are a recent thing. In the eighteenth century only around 8,000 people took holidays (Hodgkinson, 2004). The rich may have been able to spend a month in the country or conduct a grand tour of Europe. But it's only in the past hundred years that most people have received paid leave. Legislation enforcing one week's paid annual holiday was introduced in 1936. When people say they need a holiday they should remember the generations who never had a holiday – at least, not in the sense of a week away.

Our society has adopted a pattern of 48 weeks of work and four weeks of rest. We overwork for most of the year and then 'binge rest' for four weeks. But this was not the pattern for which we were made. We 'need' our holidays because our normal lives are so out of balance. The sustainable answer is not an annual holiday, but to get back to a biblical pattern of work and rest structured around a week.

It's doubtful if holidays are good for us. Eight out of ten people work extra hours before going away. One in three finds the days before a holiday the most stressful of the year.

Most say they feel as stressed as ever by the end of their first week back. When your pattern is 48 weeks work and four weeks rest then your holiday is everything. People speak of working *for* their holidays. Christmas letters typically consist of holiday itineraries. That is the sum of people's lives. Life has become week after week of toil for two weeks in the sun.

We not only spread the work–rest pattern over a year instead of a week. We spread it over a lifetime. We overwork for maybe 40 years to set up a retirement of leisure. Neither the overwork nor the retirement is healthy or godly. The Bible doesn't recognize the category of retirement. Work is to be part of life throughout life. Clearly the amount of work we can do will decrease as our capacities diminish. Nor should we equate work with employment. People may retire from employment, but still have years of active service left to give to the church or community.

The God-centred ethic: work and rest for the glory of God

The work-centred and leisure-centred ethics have their distinctive approaches to rest. With the work-centred ethic you *rest to work*. Relaxation is important because it gives the physical and emotional energy to return to work. This is the presupposition of most time management. Rest must be scheduled into your diary, we are told, because it improves your work. It's a utilitarian mechanism to revive us for more economic productivity. With the leisure-centred ethic, in contrast, you *work to rest*. Work is a necessary evil since you must earn a living, but the ultimate thing in life is leisure.

Do we rest to work or work to rest? The answer is neither. With the Bible's God-centred ethic we work for the glory of God and we rest for the glory of God. The goal is not simply a balance between work and rest. The goal for both is the glory of God. This is liberating. It gives value to both work and rest. Neither is simply a means to the other. Both are to be relished, enjoyed and used for God's glory (1 Corinthians 10:31).

Do we rest to work or work to rest? The answer is neither. With the Bible's God-centred ethic we work for the glory of God and we rest for the glory of God.

Work is not ultimate. The Sabbath day was a day to 'remember'. In a world that finds value in work and consumption, the Sabbath is a reminder that *'a man's life does not consist in the abundance of his possessions'* (Luke 12:15). Life is found in knowing God. And neither is rest ultimate. We rest for the glory of God. We enjoy the world he has made, the friendships he has provided, the abilities he has given. We enjoy them as gifts from him. More than that, we share the joy of the Creator in the world he has made. The film *Chariots of Fire* features the Scottish athlete Eric Liddell who later became a missionary to China. In the film his sister expresses concern that his running is distracting him from Christian service. Eric replies: 'I believe God made me for a purpose. But he also made me fast, and when I run I feel his pleasure.' The pleasure of walking in a bluebell wood, of stroking someone's hair, of playing hide and seek, of listening to music, of rhyme and alliteration – all bring glory to God. We 'feel his pleasure' in the world he has made. And the more so when as Christians we offer up these pleasures to God with thanks and praise. The value in such activities is not in the work they enable us to do, but in the glory they bring to God.

Whenever my father and I go on family walks one of us stuffs a tennis ball in our pockets. Then, whenever the occasion allows, we play catch. Sometimes throwing the ball hard and straight to each another; sometimes lobbing it as high as possible; sometimes standing close and simulating cricket slip catches. My transition from childhood to adulthood has done nothing to affect this practice. We're quite happy to include children in the game, but don't regard them as a necessary requirement. I was reminded of this when I read Calvin Seerveld's book *Rainbows for the Fallen World*. He asks: 'Is playing catch no longer redeeming the time after you reach twenty, unless you do it with your children?' (Seerveld, 1980).

In Proverbs 8, Wisdom is personified and her role in creation described. The New Testament identifies Wisdom as Jesus Christ, through whom God created the world. The passage in Proverbs 8 ends: *'Then I was the craftsman at his side. I was filled with delight day after day, rejoicing always in his presence, rejoicing in his whole world and delighting in mankind'* (Proverbs 8:30–31). The word translated 'rejoice' means laughter or play. Seerveld translates it: 'I was enjoying myself day after day, playing around all the time in front of God's face, playing through the hemispheres of his earth, having fun with all of mankind'. God was being playful in creation. He was having fun. Through play we participate in this divine creative joy. We share God's delight in the world he has made. Play will be part of life in the new creation (Jeremiah 30:18–19; 31:4, 13–14; Zechariah 8:5). Sometimes playfulness is part of work, like the pleasure of a well-crafted piece of wood, a well-constructed sentence or a flourishing garden. Sometimes it takes place in the context of work, like workplace banter or jokes. Sometimes it is its own independent activity, like throwing a ball around in the park. In any context, when consecrated by faith in the Creator and prayerful thankfulness, it brings glory to God (1 Timothy 4:4–5).

3. USE YOUR TIME EFFICIENTLY

We've seen that there's nothing wrong with being busy. The truth is most of us like being busy. Worse than being busy is having nothing to do – even if in times of stress doing nothing may seem very attractive. Busyness itself is not a problem. In anybody's life there will be periods of intense activity. The problem comes when we are persistently over-busy. If your life doesn't reflect the biblical pattern of work and rest then something is wrong. We don't mind being busy, but not *this* busy!

I'm assuming you've picked up this book because you want to do something about your busyness. Or maybe you want to help others who are busy. I want to suggest four key steps to addressing busyness:

Step One: Use your time efficiently.
Step Two: Sort out your priorities.
Step Three: Glorify God all the time.

Step Four: Identify the desires of your heart that make
              you try to do more than God expects of you.

Using time efficiently is the discipline of time management.
Sometimes we're busy because we don't manage our time
well. This is only ever part of the problem, but it can be a contributing factor. There are things we can do to use our time
more efficiently. There's no need to give time management
advice a Christian gloss. This is the sort of wisdom the writer
of Proverbs would have been pleased to endorse. Within the
created order there are patterns of cause and effect. Many
of these unbelievers and believers alike can observe. *The plans
of the diligent lead to profit as surely as haste leads to poverty'*
(Proverbs 21:5). So this chapter contains some time management advice. It won't solve your busyness problem, but it may
help. Some of what I say relates mainly to work, some to the
home. As you read, make a list of ideas that you want to put
into practice.

Which of the following statements apply to you?

- ☐ I often pick up paperwork and then put it down again to
  deal with later.
- ☐ I prefer to do most things myself rather than ask
  someone else to do them.
- ☐ I don't have a clear sense of what I need to do at the
  start of each day.
- ☐ I often spend several minutes looking for
  something.
- ☐ My meetings often last longer than they need to.
- ☐ I often find myself rushing to meet deadlines.
- ☐ I start projects that I never finish.
- ☐ I put off tasks I don't enjoy.
- ☐ I don't know where my TV licence is.

If you didn't tick any boxes then you can skip this chapter
– further proof that good time management saves time!

Try keeping a time log for the next few days. Write down
how you spend your time at work and at home. Log the task, its
duration, whether it was planned or not, and an assessment of
whether its value was high, medium or low. Don't just judge the
value of tasks simply by their pay-off to you. Christ commands
you to love God and love your neighbour (Mark 12:29–31). Judge
the value of your activities by these two criteria. After a few
days review your time log.

- Over how much of your time did you have some
  measure of control?
- How much of your time was productive?
- Did your use of time reflect your priorities?
- Why did you spend time on tasks of little value?
- What did you do that was a waste of time?
- How much of your time was planned?
- Did many of your planned activities take longer than
  expected?
- Were interruptions valuable? If not, could they have
  been avoided?
- Were you doing tasks that it would have been better for
  other people to do?
- What time of day is most productive for you?
- Would you describe your lifestyle as one with work–life
  balance?
- Are reading the Bible and prayer part of your daily
  routine?

A little bit of planning

I border on the obsessive when it comes to planning and organization. There's no moral virtue in this – it's just who I am and

other people are different. You need to find a way of planning your time that works for you – that fits both your lifestyle and personality. But you will need to work at it. It might involve learning new habits. I remember a conversation with one of my tutors at university. He told me he always knew what he would be doing during the next day because he planned his time. At the time I was astonished. I could be busy (though, of course, I was a student), but I decided what to do as I went along. What astonishes me now is that I was astonished at the time.

Break down large projects into achievable steps and then set aside time for each step. I have a document on my computer with a table or grid. Down the left-hand side are the main tasks that face me. Some are one-offs like writing a book on busyness. Others are ongoing like leading a church plant. Across the top are the months of the year. I break down projects into steps and allocate them to different months. Every month I list the tasks in that month's column. I know that if I do those tasks in that month then I'll be on track to finish my projects. I also have a row for one-off events I need to remember, like servicing the car, plus a row for birthdays.

Spend five minutes planning at the beginning or end of each day. Work out your priorities for the coming day. Don't fill the whole day, as every day contains the unexpected. Remember, too, that few of us correctly predict how long tasks will take – half as long again as we think they will take is a good rule of thumb. The key thing is to look ahead. Don't be preoccupied with immediate deadlines. What preparation is needed for forthcoming activities? What do you need to do to achieve long-term goals? People talk about 'helicopter vision' – the ability to rise above the everyday routine to review the past and look ahead.

Do priority items first – not the fun stuff. Or leave important items to a quiet point in the day. Do similar activities together – things like phoning, correspondence, filing or household chores. If you're not good in the mornings then make your packed lunch, choose your clothes and pack your bag the night before. Start working on a creative project well in advance, even if it's just to write down some initial thoughts. That way ideas can brew away in the back of your mind. For example, I'll look at a Bible passage I'm going to preach on two or three weeks ahead of time. That way I can reflect on it in idle moments or I might spot a great illustration while listening to the news. Spend time saving time. Ever been too busy to read an instruction manual only to find half an hour later that reading it would have saved you time? Short cuts can take longer. Be prepared to make the most of 'dead time'. Take sermon tapes on long car journeys or a book to read while you wait for your doctor's appointments. A friend who is a school teacher managed to do much of his MBA course in 'dead time'. It's also a great opportunity to pray – even if it's just the time it takes for the lift to move between floors.

I was once involved in a major change management project at work. Right at the beginning my colleague Julian said something that has always stuck with me: 'If you don't make a plan then you won't know what to change.' In other words, plans can't be set in stone. They have to be tinkered with all the time. In fact plans help you adjust to delays, interruptions and crises. I change my monthly plan several times each day. If a pastoral issue comes up then I don't need to fret about what I've left undone. I simply reschedule. A plan should be your servant not your master. And make sure your plan is portable. If it's not to hand you won't be able use it to manage your time.

Taming paperwork

Handle documents, letters and emails only once. Don't pick something up, look it over and then put it down to deal with another time. Either act on it, file it or bin it. Pay bills straight away or, better still, set up a direct debit. Don't use your in-tray as storage space and don't place it close to where you work so that it distracts you. If it's in your eye-line you'll always be tempted to pick up the top item rather than get stuck into a difficult task. And don't leave your email software constantly running for the same reason. Sort out the papers in your briefcase every day. Keep your desk clear so you're not distracted by papers on your desk.

Think about what you can do to reduce unproductive paper-work and emails. You may have a secretary or PA who can screen stuff for you. I used to block all corporate emails, leaving it to my PA to tell me if anything important came round – a rare occurrence! Ask for a verbal update rather than a written one. In the UK you can register free with the Telephone Preference Service (www.tpsonline.org.uk) and the Mailing Preference Service (www.mpsonline.org.uk) to bar unsolic-ited marketing phone calls and junk mail.

Only read journals, magazines and newsgroups that have a proven record of providing you with information you need. Look through the contents and go straight to the sections you need. Look for summaries, diagrams and conclusions, or skim through documents to get key headings. When you write documents do so with the reader in mind. Make their life easier by writing clearly with good headings and summar-ies. One participant in a writing skills course I was running was startled by my suggestion that good writing might be considered an act of love for our neighbours at work.

Eighty-five percent of filed information is never used again – a waste of time and space. So try to bin most of that 85% before it reaches your files! Every time you go into your files looking for something, take the opportunity to do a bit of purging. If you see a document you don't need, bin it straight away. Forty-five percent of filing is already stored somewhere else. So you could try the filing method used by a team in one of my previous workplaces. They knew their line manager was an assiduous filer. So they copied him in on any documents they thought they might need again. Then they threw everything away. They had no filing at all. If they ever needed anything they simply asked his secretary for a copy. For household paperwork, buy a few A4 folders and label them: utilities, tax, car, bank, and so on. Just stuff the latest bill or letter in the front when you've dealt with it and it'll always be easy to find it again.

Every time you make a list or set of instructions, keep a copy on your computer if you have one. Your Christmas card list, travel directions for visitors, or instructions for looking after your pet, for example. Keep a list of items to pack when you go on holiday. It'll take a bit more effort the first time round (although you can find sample ones on the internet), but saves time from then on. It also relieves all the fretting about what you might have forgotten. You can revise it with every holiday. Put everything down on the list – you can simply skip 'sun cream' when you go for a winter break in Scotland.

Managing people

Most managers spend between 30% and 50% of their time in meetings. Always ask yourself whether meetings are really necessary. Could the business be conducted through a phone call or email instead? Keep project or committee papers in one file; then you can just pick up that file when you head off for a meeting. Arrive on time. I used to fill the time between the scheduled start of a meeting and the actual start time by calculating the cost to the organization of the late start. Guess the average salary of those attending, work out what that is per minute, multiply it by the number of people attending the meeting and so on. If you don't have time to work it out then your meeting hasn't started too late – either that or you need to brush up your arithmetic. Contribute constructively and focus on the meeting's objectives. Don't just think about using your time well, but everyone else's too.

If you are chairing a meeting, then start on time. If you wait until everyone's ready, people will turn up late next time to save the time they wasted previously by coming on time. Chair the meeting in a style that meets its objectives. If it's for communication then keep participation to a minimum. If it's a brainstorming meeting then let the discussion flow. Restrict contributions to agenda items and be clear about any follow-up steps to be taken and who will take responsibility for them.

Interruptions can waste your time. Try saying something like: 'I'm busy at the moment, can we talk later?' Ask someone to come to the point. You don't have to be rude. 'How can I help you?' usually does the trick. But be careful: interruptions often turn out to be central to your main responsibilities. I often tell myself that as a pastor my job is to teach people the Bible and help them apply it to their lives. So when someone comes to me with a problem that sends my schedule out the window, I remind myself that I'm actually doing what's central to my role. Signal that a meeting is coming to an end by saying something like, 'Before we finish . . .'. Standing up will let someone know their time with you is over. We have friends who say to Christian guests who have overstayed their welcome: 'Shall we pray before you leave?'

Just because a telephone rings doesn't mean you have to answer it. Set aside a quiet hour in which you won't take calls, and always put calls on hold during meetings. Screen calls by putting on the answering machine. Take a moment before you phone someone to think through what you want to cover and achieve. It may be appropriate to summarize at the end and agree actions as if it were a mini-meeting. At home or at the office, a list of useful numbers by the phone saves time.

When you delegate tasks communicate clearly what needs to be done and give all the information needed together with a deadline. Mess this up and time will be wasted. And then let go of the task. Don't just delegate tasks; delegate authority as well, so people can get on with it without referring back to you all the time. Thank people for their work and don't simply dump tasks on others.

Around the house
Some people like to do all the cleaning at one time, but most people find it easier to do a little each day. You might find it helpful to have one set task a day: washing on Monday, ironing on Tuesday, big shop on Wednesday and so on. Some tasks like ironing are quicker if you do it all in one go. Although – other than shirts, blouses, trousers and dresses – how much ironing does anyone really need to do?

Organize your home so everything is where you're most likely to use it. Tea, coffee, sugar and mugs should all be near the kettle. Keep your hair brush next to the mirror. Put together a collection of everyday recipes. By all means have fun flicking through your fancy cookbooks when you have a dinner party. But most of us use a range of easy, cheap every-day meals. Collating these also helps when you're deciding what to cook. Sometimes you can cook twice as much as you need and freeze half for another day.

Keep a list of grocery needs in your kitchen. Try to get your family to write items on it every time they finish something off. I've arranged our list with headings that correspond to the supermarket (fruit and veg, meat, fridge and so on). It saves wandering all over the supermarket. My wife was scornful at first, but she's become a convert! It also means less impulse buying of products you don't really need. Buy greeting cards in bulk so you always have one when you discover at the last minute that it's someone's birthday. And buy Christmas presents throughout the year whenever you see something that a particular person might like.

Don't spend more time organizing than you need to. One book on time management I read had 44 sample forms! What am I supposed to do with a 'wardrobe inventory'? You don't need to line up socks in your sock drawer! Most drawers can be higgledy-piggledly because you'll just reach in to grab what you need.

What does waste time is having to search in several possible locations, so have a set place for things. A few boxes or plastic tubs will help your storage. Again, each box need not be tidy inside. It's enough to know which box something will be in. As your parents no doubt used to tell you, put things back from where you got them. Drop your keys in a basket in the hallway as you come in and you'll always know where to find them. Unless you have an artistic flair for such things, don't label food jars when it's obvious what's inside. I don't need a label telling me the long, thin stuff in the glass jar is spaghetti!

'Finish what's on your plate – think of the poor children in Africa' has always struck me as a very bogus piece of moral reasoning. I doubt the patronized 'children of Africa' want my leftover sprouts packaged up and posted to them. What benefit they derive from our over-eating is difficult to say. But some people seem to apply a similar logic to household clutter. Somehow it is morally improper to throw things away. In fact the best course is to get rid of as many things as possible. If they work then pass them on or give them to a charity shop. Broken or obsolete items should be chucked.

The real moral imperative is not to buy stuff you won't use much in the first place. Don't succumb to fads, envy, or the idolatrous practice of shopping simply to feel good.

Get your children to help with household chores. This doesn't actually save you time, but it's an important part of preparing your children for life.

By now you may have a list of things you want to put into practice plus a few ideas of your own. I suggest you reread the chapter in a few weeks time. How are you getting on? Are there ideas you missed?

1. People not schedules

I want to end with three warnings not to let time management get out of control. The problem with schedules is they easily become ends in themselves. They should be the means that enable us efficiently to use time and so serve others. 'The practice of time management is actually relationship management within the arena of time' (Andrew, 2002). But our schedule can become a greater priority than people. This seems a particular problem for Anglo-Saxons. Other cultures value people over schedules. A friend of mine once visited the wrong house by mistake, but still its Pakistani occupant invited him in. He stayed for nearly an hour even though, as he later learned, the man had been just about to go to work. It's possible to run an efficient meeting that keeps to time, sticks to the point and cuts out chat and banter. But chat and banter are the heart and soul of relationships. And

> *The problem with schedules is they easily become ends in themselves. They should be the means that enable us efficiently to use time and so serve others.*

relationships are the oil that makes organizations run smoothly. You can't work together as a team without good relationships. Don't confuse efficiency and effectiveness.

Busyness can also be a way of avoiding time for people. 'I'm busy' is sometimes a euphemism for 'back off'. Our schedules can be an excuse for not serving others. 'I'd love to help,' we say, 'but I'm tied up this week.' It's very easy to set yourself tasks for the day and for these to become more important than the person we meet in need. In an experiment, theology students were told to go to another building on campus to give a talk on the Good Samaritan (Darley and Batson, 1973). On the way was an actor simulating pain and distress. Those who thought they had plenty of time stopped to help. Most of those who were told they were late ignored the man in their haste to be on time to talk about the Good Samaritan.

2. Servant not master

Plans and schedules are good servants, but they are poor masters. We can use our schedules to control our lives instead of being ruled by God. We can trust our time management instead of trusting God's care. We can turn the good desire for order into an idol. And idols have a habit of turning the tables on us. They end up controlling us. This is how the Lilliputians in Jonathan Swift's novel *Gulliver's Travels* describe Gulliver's watch:

> Out of the right fob hung a great silver chain, with a wonderful kind of engine at the bottom . . . He put this engine to our ears, which made an incessant noise like that of a watermill. And we conjecture it is either some unknown animal, or the god that he worships: but we are more inclined to the latter opinion, because he assured us (if we understood him right, for he expressed himself very imperfectly), that he seldom did anything without

consulting it. He called it his oracle, and said it pointed out the time for every action of his life.

Why not take the scenic route home? If your god is your schedule then a longer route home will be irksome. But if your God is the God who made the heavens and the earth, and pronounced them good, then the scenic route home will be a chance to share his verdict on what he has made.

3. Eternity not time

The Christian writer Hannah More once showed a visitor what she called her 'moral prospect'. It was possible to stand looking out of her kitchen window in such a way that a few nearby bushes obscured a large forest in the distance. 'So the things of time, being near,' she commented, 'seem great and so hide from our view the things of eternity.' One of the dangers of time management is that it focuses our attention on the immediate. But the immediate is not always, or even often, the important. God made days. Hours, minutes and seconds are human inventions. There are no words for seconds or minutes in our Bibles. '"How to get 26 hours out of every day" (the title of a recent work on time management) would have meant nothing to Jesus and the Bible writers,' says Tony Payne (Payne, 2001). 'They didn't divide the day into 24 hours and they just didn't think about time as a thing to be spent or wasted or maximized or organized.' The Bible tells us to number our days, not schedule our minutes. And numbering our days means to live in the light of eternity. Over the triple doorways of Milan Cathedral are three inscriptions. Over one is carved a beautiful wreath of roses with the inscription: 'All that pleases is but for a moment.' Over the second is a cross with the words: 'All that troubles is but for a moment.' Over the central doorway are the words: 'That only is important which is eternal.'

I have suggested that using time efficiently is the first step to sorting out busyness. Good time management advice has a contribution to make. But it is the *least* important step. That's because:

- *What* you do matters more than how much you do. That's why the second step is: Sort out your priorities.
- *How* you do it matters more than how much you do. That's why the third step is: Glorify God all the time.
- *Why* you do it matters more than how much you do. That's why the fourth step is: Identify the desires of your heart that make you try to do more than God expects of you.

4. SORT OUT YOUR PRIORITIES

'Stop wasting time.' 'Hurry up.' 'Get a move on.' These are the commands by which we condition children to accept our scheduled view of time. I have a dreamy daughter who easily gets preoccupied. She'll play with the water when she should be having a wash; play imaginary games when she should be getting dressed; examine a flower when she should be walking to school. It saddens me how often I hurry out of her playfulness to meet the schedules of life.

Wasting time or redeeming time

Yet Paul tells us to *'redeem the time'* in Ephesians 5:16 and Colossians 4:5. *'Make the most of every opportunity'* is how the NIV translates it. On the face of it this appears to suggest there is no time for wasting time in the Christian life. 'Hurry up,' should be our cry as we rush from one activity to the next. But it's important to look at what Paul says in context. In Ephesians 5:15–16 Paul says: *'Be very careful, then, how you live*

– not as unwise but as wise, making the most of every opportunity, because the days are evil.' The reason we're to redeem the time is *'because the days are evil'*. The word Paul uses is not the word meaning duration of time in years and days (*chronos*). It's the word for a specific time of opportunity or crisis (*kairos*). Paul has been talking about those who live in darkness and whose deeds are darkness. But the light of God's new world is dawning (verses 3–14). So to redeem the time is not to fill our days with activity. It's a call to live as children of light. We are to live in a way appropriate for the time in which we live, and the time in which Christians live is the coming new age that is breaking into the darkness. It is about *what* we do, not *how much* we do. We redeem that time by living in the light – staying sober, being filled with the Spirit, singing God's word to one another, submitting to one another (verses 17–21). If you don't have time to *'make music in your heart to the Lord'* then you aren't redeeming the time (verse 19). The Puritan Richard Baxter (1615–1691) said: 'Spend your time in nothing which you know must be repented of; in nothing on which you might not pray for the blessing of God; in nothing which you could not review with a quiet conscience on your dying bed; in nothing which you might not safely and properly be found doing if death should surprise you in the act.'

In Colossians 4:5–6 the context is different. *'Be wise in the way you act towards outsiders; make the most of every opportunity. Let your conversation be always full of grace, seasoned with salt, so that you may know how to answer everyone.'* Again it's not about how much we do. It's about seizing opportunities to share the gospel when they arise in conversation. And the main threat to this is not that we are idling on the sofa, but that we fear other people. That's why Paul asks for prayer that he might have boldness to proclaim the gospel as he should (verse 4). In order to make the most of every opportunity we have to have time to chat with unbelievers. And people don't talk about personal or spiritual issues in a hurry. It takes time because it takes trust. You may have to chew the cud on football, politics and television soaps for quite a while before someone will talk about their sin and their need of forgiveness.

So good time management is not about squeezing more into life. It is about making sure you do what is important for you to do. It's about, as the management guru Stephen Covey says, 'putting first things first'. It's not about shaving off a few minutes here and there or having your time so planned that 'interruptions' become a problem. So, while step one in sorting out our busyness was *use your time efficiently*, step two is *sort out your priorities*. Unless you're lazy, you can't do new things without stopping other activities. Covey asks: 'What one thing could you do (that you aren't doing now) that if you did it on a regular basis would make a tremendously positive difference to your life?' Take a moment to answer that question for yourself.

Why aren't you doing it already?

Putting the kingdom of God first

In the Sermon on the Mount Jesus said: '*Seek first [God's] kingdom and his righteousness*' (Matthew 6:33). Putting first things first means putting the kingdom of God first. It means being gospel-centred. Consider the following statements from Jesus and Paul:

> *I have brought you glory on earth by completing the work you gave me to do* (John 17:4).

> *So from Jerusalem all the way around to Illyricum, I have fully proclaimed the gospel of Christ* (Romans 15:19).

I have fought the good fight, I have finished the race, I have kept the faith
(2 Timothy 4:7).

Both Jesus and Paul could say at the end of their lives that
they had completed the job. Their lives were not too short –
though both of them died early, unnatural deaths. They had
enough time. Think about that for a moment. Think about
how many people were left unhealed; how many mouths
were unfed; how many people didn't hear the gospel; how
many towns where churches were not planted.

Jesus and Paul could speak of completing the work not
because they had completed a defined task, but because they
had worked faithfully throughout their lives. Paul doesn't say
he has won the fight, but that he has stuck at the job of fighting. It's not that Paul had finished the job and was looking
forward to retirement. It was rather than he had been faithful
to the ministry God gave him. What mattered to Paul was finishing the race, not finishing the 'to-do list'. The 'success' of
our lives will be measured not in what we have 'achieved', but
in our faithfulness.

In John's account of Jesus' death we read: *'Later, knowing
that all was now completed* [= accomplished], *and so that the
Scripture would be fulfilled* [= accomplished], *Jesus said, "I am
thirsty." A jar of wine vinegar was there, so they soaked a sponge in
it, put the sponge on a stalk of the hyssop plant, and lifted it to Jesus'
lips. When he had received the drink, Jesus said, "It is finished* [=
accomplished]." *With that, he bowed his head and gave up his
spirit'* (John 19:28–30). John has a word he usually uses to say
the Scriptures are fulfilled, but here he uses a different word.
It is the same word as 'completed' and 'finished' in verses 28
and 30. Jesus knew his work was finished because he had done
all that was spoken of him in the Old Testament. The word of
God defined the task of Jesus. And, while Jesus' work in salva-

tion was unique, the word of God also defines our task. Our priority is to live faithfully in the light of God's word.

Sometimes, when my wife asks me if I've had a productive day, I reply: 'It depends whether you're talking about what I've done or what I've still got to do.' We can start the day with a list of things to do and by the end of the day everything's still on it plus a few more items besides! It's tempting to think the day has been a failure and the solution is to be busier. But the question to ask is not 'What have I got left to do?' Instead you should ask: 'Have I used my time well? Have I worked hard to serve others and glorify God?'

'Jesus did not finish all the urgent tasks in Palestine,' comments Robert Banks (1983), 'nor all the things he would have liked to do. But he did finish the work God gave him to do. So can we.' In John 17:4 Jesus talks of *'completing the work'* the Father gave him. In John 4:34 he uses the same phrase to describe the food which satisfies him: *'"My food," said Jesus, "is to do the will of him who sent me and to finish his work".'* The disciples had left him to find food, but he has been 'fed' by talking to the Samaritan woman. He goes on to speak of the fields being ready for harvest. This is the task that has been given to us, but in that task *'one sows and another reaps'* (John 4:37). We each have different roles – the whole task doesn't belong to any of us. This is how we should understand Paul's claim to *'have fully proclaimed the gospel of Christ'* in Romans 15:19. C. E. B. Cranfield (1975) says: 'We understand his claim to have completed the gospel of Christ to be a claim to have completed that trail-blazing, pioneer preaching of it, which he believed it was his own special apostolic mission to accomplish.'

To summarize:

- 'Success' is about faithfulness not how much we have done.

- We are to be faithful to the task of making Jesus known
  – a task shared by all Christians.
- We are to be faithful to the specific ministry that we
  have because of the gifts and opportunities that God
  gives to us.

But proper 'time management' starts by asking what we're doing. It's about getting a clear sense of inner direction rather than an external schedule.

Time management emphasizes efficient use of time. It's about accumulating extra time by eradicating time wasting. But proper 'time management' starts by asking *what* we're doing. It's about getting a clear sense of inner direction rather than an external schedule. It's about 'putting first things first' and that means putting first the kingdom of God. For busy people this is what discipleship means.

Putting the kingdom of God first in practice

Most of us organize our lives in the following way.

| lifestyle | ⇨ | job | ⇨ | home | ⇨ | church | ⇨ | ministry |

The first stage is to decide on the **lifestyle** we will live. In reality, though, we don't really decide this. What we do is mimic the values of the world. We adopt the lifestyles of our friends, neighbours and colleagues. As a result our standard of living is pretty much like everyone else's. In order to achieve this lifestyle we look for a **job** with a salary that will fund our aspirations. Of course we don't always get the job and salary we would like, but what we're after is clear: the job that funds the lifestyle. And so we try to get on in our careers. When we get the job, we look for a **home** nearby. And when we find a home we look for a local **church** that suits us. And maybe when we've found a church to our liking, we might get involved in some way. At the end of the line we decide what kind of Christian **ministry** we might do. People rarely work through this chain in a premeditated way, but one decision leads to another in our lives. Nor will the model describe everyone. But the key point is this: lifestyle, job and home (in whatever order) come before church and ministry. This is *leftover discipleship*. My time for Christian ministry and Christian community comes from whatever is left over at the end of the week.

There is another model, a more biblical model. Jesus says: *'Do not set your heart on what you will eat or drink; do not worry about it. For the pagan world runs after all such things, and your Father knows that you need them. But seek his kingdom, and these things will be given to you as well'* (Luke 12:29–31). We stop adopting the lifestyle of the world around us – what Jesus calls running after the things the pagan world runs after. We refuse to be shaped by the values of the world (Romans 12:2). You might consider the following exercise:

1. List the values, priorities and aspirations of our culture. Think about the priorities found in adverts, magazines, television programmes and among your peers.
2. List your own values, priorities and aspirations.
3. Read Luke's Gospel and list the values, priorities and aspirations of Jesus.
4. Compare the lists.

Saying 'No' to the pattern of this world frees us to reverse the process. We start by putting first the kingdom of God. We start with church and ministry.

Work out your ministry priorities by asking the following sorts of questions:

- What are the gifts and abilities that God has given to me?
- What do I enjoy doing?
- Who do I want to reach or serve?
- What needs are there that I can meet?
- What opportunities are there for ministry?
- With whom can I work?

None of the answers to these questions on their own will determine your priorities. Focusing on gifts and enjoyment in isolation can lead to people being self-centred and indulgent. Paul stresses the different gifts God gives to emphasize how we need one another (Romans 12 and 1 Corinthians 12), not to encourage us to find fulfilment in only doing what we enjoy. 'Ministry' is just another word for 'service'. So ministry is not about self-fulfilment. It's about serving others in love in whatever way is appropriate. So deciding your priorities should be a community activity. Your priorities will be affected by those of your church and vice versa. Other Christians will have a good sense of what you should focus on. The key thing is to build your life around your ministry and your commitment to your church. That doesn't mean only doing 'churchy' things. Your priority may be serving God in the workplace or neighbourhood. But you'll see this as part of the wider ministry of your church. Some people find it helpful to come up with a personal 'mission statement' – a brief summary of their priorities in life (Sine and Sine, 2002).

With your church and ministry thought through, you then look for a home near the church and perhaps one that helps you do your ministry to the full. Then you look for a job that allows you to do your ministry. What counts is no longer the Western dream, but serving God and putting first his kingdom. So instead of leftovers service, we have a leftovers lifestyle. We'll be content with whatever standard of living allows us to serve God. Discipleship means living for Jesus and letting everything else fit around that.

It's not just as individuals that we need constantly to be refocusing on the gospel. We may need to 'downsize' the activities of church to create space for gospel relationships. Fruit trees need to be pruned if they're to be fruitful. It may be that your church needs a good pruning. Steve Croft (2002) comments:

> Many (if not all) local churches tend to run at slightly more than their capacity in terms of the energy of their ministers and active members. There is often so much going on that what fruit there might be is choked and does not reach maturity because there is no space for it to grow. The reasons for this overcrowding and lack of pruning are many and various. Projects are easier to begin than to close down in the life of the local church. None of us like conflict . . . The pruning knife needs to be taken to the tree before good things will grow again. Space needs to be created, with love and care. We need to practise subtraction before we can do addition. We need to do less, well in order to achieve more.

Time for myself

'I need some "me-time",' we say, 'some time for myself; I've had a hard week so I've earned some time to indulge myself.' Some people are extroverts. They're energized by spending time with people. Other people are introverts. They recharge in quiet and solitude. Most of us are somewhere in the middle. We all need to do some things on our own. But most people's idea of 'time to myself' is time to pamper oneself. Time alone is good, but not when it overrides responsibility. There's a difference between time alone and time for self. We don't 'find' ourselves on our own. When God made humanity he said: '"Let us make man in our image, in our likeness, and let them rule over the fish of the sea and the birds of the air, over the livestock, over all the earth, and over all the creatures that move along the ground." So God created man in his own image, in the image of God he created him; male and female he created them' (Genesis 1:26–27).

Notice first that God said 'Let us'. God is a triune community of three persons in eternal relationship. The divine persons are defined by their relationship with one another. The Father is the Father because he has a Son. And we are made in the image of the triune God. We often think of individuality as being 'different from other people'. But true personhood is found through relationships. Just as a mother is a mother because she has children so I am a person because I have relationships. We don't find ourselves on our own. We find ourselves through relationships (see Chester, 2005).

Second, being made in the image of God means sharing his loving rule over creation. We were made to serve God and other people. We find ourselves not through 'me-time', but through service. Our priority is to love God and our neighbours. Jesus tells us how we 'find' ourselves: 'Whoever wants to save his life will lose it, but whoever loses his life for me and for the gospel will save it' (Mark 8:35). We find ourselves by losing our lives. We are called to balance work and rest. But we are not called to balance service and self-indulgence. You were bought with a price (1 Corinthians 6:19–20). All of your life is now to be lived for Christ's glory and in his service.

Time for my family

Often family and church are portrayed as being in tension. No doubt there are times when families need to be alone together. But what are your aspirations for your children? This is where the rubber hits the road. People speak about putting the kingdom first, but in practice it's often second to their children. 'I'd work on that difficult estate,' people say, 'but it wouldn't be fair on my children.' And we all nod wisely as if this is self-evident. But it's highly questionable. I shocked someone recently by asking them to name one occasion on which Jesus speaks positively about families. Every time Jesus talks about families he sees them as competing for our loyalty to him and his community.

I heard recently of a couple who are so busy with their careers they barely see each other or their children during the week. And at weekends they're so stressed that family relationships are inevitably frayed. Yet they justify this in the name of their children. Their hard work means their children are learning to ski by the age of seven and recently spent three weeks in Brazil. The problem is that they may already be in too deep: the top of the range cars, the business class flights and the beautiful home are not going to be easy to give up.

Whatever we say about ourselves, our true values come to the surface in our aspirations for our children. Do you hope your children will be comfortable and well-paid? Or do you hope they will be radical, risk-taking gospel workers? If it's the latter then what better way to further that end than by modelling it for them? And not only modelling it, but involving them in it. What does family time actually mean? Watching the television, eating Big Macs, trips to the shopping centre? What values do these reinforce? What about making the service of others what unites us as families? What about weekly times when the whole family does something together for the good of others?

5. GLORIFY GOD ALL THE TIME

How can Christians serve God when their lives are so busy? One answer is to question the premise of such a question. It suggests that serving God is a different kind of activity from all the other things that fill our lives. Serving God looks like preaching, visiting the sick or running a youth group. It doesn't look like driving a van, completing accounts or repairing an engine. We want to do something for God, but we confine this to our spare time or 'full-time Christian ministry'. A Christian legal secretary once wrote to me: 'Can I content myself with the philosophy that all of life is ministry and whatever I do for the glory of God is fine? How then do I answer people who think if I'm not leading a Bible study I'm not a gospel minister?' A speech therapist wrote: 'I often fall into the trap of devaluing work to the point that it's only to earn money to enable other gospel work and living. What's the point of spending your whole week in secular employment?'

But in the biblical worldview all of life – 'ordinary' life – can and should be lived for God's glory. We struggle to find time for God when in fact *all* of our time can be lived with him and for him. We feel guilty about not doing more as Christians when we are already spending 24 hours a day as Christians. As Elizabeth Elliot puts it: 'My house, my kitchen, my desk, my very body are meant to be holy places in this world for the eternal God.' Ordinary life is the theatre of God's glory. God and work don't have to make competing demands. We can serve God in and through our work.

So the third step to addressing our over-busyness is this: *glorify God all the time*. It's intended as much as a word of comfort and freedom as a word of exhortation. You don't have to get up at four o'clock and eat breakfast while you clean your teeth while you dictate memos while you read the paper while you travel to work just so you find a bit more time to serve God. Your whole life can be offered to him for his glory. Let's suppose you spend 10% of your waking hours reading the Bible, praying, sharing the gospel, supporting your church, discipling other Christians. That's 10% of your time. But if you glorify God all the time, you've immediately increased that to 100%. We've just gained another 14 or 15 hours a day to serve God. Result!

If you wanted to be spiritual what would you do? Most of us, I suspect, would think of praying or singing; perhaps reading the Bible. We would think of activities that we do away from the world of ordinary life. Spirituality in our minds is about withdrawal. It takes place in some inner world. Retreat centres are always based in the countryside, presumably because God is assumed to be closer in the quiet of the country. The very notion of 'retreat' suggests withdrawal from ordinary life. But this is bourgeois spirituality for middle-class people with the time and money to get away from it all. What does it offer the single parent living in a tower block or the harassed executive checking his emails at home? David Prior says: 'Despite our personal and corporate efforts to lead a spiritual life, we do not sense the presence of God in our work. The problem is that we have developed a spirituality that is based on an experience of God *elsewhere* – in our withdrawal from the marketplace rather than in it' (Parmiter, 2005).

We value the extraordinary over the ordinary. Whether it's conferences, spiritual experiences, revivals – we are looking for the extraordinary. But Jesus conducted his ministry in the context of meals, journeys and homes. Everyday tasks – washing up, waiting in traffic, using the photocopier – can be occasions for prayer or Bible meditation. Why not write out a verse and pull it from your pocket in idle moments? Why not use emails and phone calls as prompts to pray for people? Next time you're stuck in a traffic jam or waiting for your computer to unfreeze, think of it as an opportunity to grow in humility and patience. Reflect on God's sovereign love at work sometimes through our plans, but often contrary to them.

Jesus conducted his ministry in the context of meals, journeys and homes. Everyday tasks – washing up, waiting in traffic, using the photocopier – can be occasions for prayer or Bible meditation.

Changing a nappy, clearing up in an old people's home, working on a supermarket checkout – these activities can be transformed if we gain a sense of serving others in obedience to God. Michael Card (1993) writes: 'The cry of a baby in the middle of the night is not simply a summons to change a nappy – it contains within it more than our ears can hear. It is a call to leave the cosy self-interest of our warm beds; to come, saying no to a thousand voices that tell us to remain where we are comfortable. It is a call to come away from ourselves. No one who has ever heeded this call will tell you it was in vain.'

Many think the goal of spirituality is serenity and stillness. But the goal of biblical spirituality is conformity to Christ. It is to deny yourself, take up your cross and follow him. And the cross was not a place of serenity. It was a place of selflessness and sacrificial love in the midst of hate and violence. Every client, every customer, every colleague presents us with an opportunity to show love.

So this chapter is about glorifying God in 'ordinary' life – especially in our work. My friend Rob, a financial adviser and church planter, once wrote to me: 'I think there is a danger that the value of full-time work and the energy it requires is underestimated. The value of it is both in terms of having gospel witness in the workplace, and in terms of the financial support that it can provide to the gospel ministry of others. For these two reasons alone, it is about as important an activity as I can think of doing.'

We should take delight in our work just as God takes delight in his work

The world has come about because God is a worker. And God is still a worker. When the Bible tells us God rested from his work, it is only his work of creation. Jesus says: '*My Father is always at his work to this very day, and I, too, am working*' (John 5:17). God is a worker and Jesus is a worker (John 4:34 and 17:4). And God takes delight in his work. He looks at what he has done and says, 'It is good'. The Christian understanding of creation teaches us that work is something in which we should take delight just as God delights in his work (Proverbs 8:30–31).

Not only is God a worker, but he makes humanity to share his work. We are made in God's image to rule over God's world (Genesis 1:27–28). God placed humanity '*in the Garden of Eden to work it and take care of it*' (Genesis 2:15). God created the world as a good, but unfinished, project. He called on humanity to fill it and subdue it. This is often called 'the cultural mandate'. God gives us a mandate to create, invent, explore, discover, develop, produce, buy and sell. God graciously invites us to participate with him in the task of producing a beautiful world that brings him glory. A Christian businessman once said to me:

> In much Christian teaching the value of your work is only seen in moments of proclamation because work itself is not ministry. There is nothing on making a difference at work through work. Or else value is given to jobs that affect quality of life through public service (teachers, nurses), but not wealth creation. Many working Christians have no positive feedback at the end of the day; no moral vision for wealth creation as that which pays for the health service as well as gospel ministry.

So work is commended in the Bible as a good thing. That's why we find satisfaction and fulfilment in work. To work is part of what it means to be human. Through work we provide for our families and contribute to our communities (Deuteronomy 14:28–29; Ephesians 4:28). Studies have shown that workers increase their output if they believe their work to be important and significant. We find pleasure in a product well made or a service well performed – something that works, something that is beautiful, something that will endure. The craftsman runs his hand over the smoothed wood with delight and pride. It's a pleasure that we can all find in our work: the clean floor, the student who grasps an idea, the empty in-tray, the satisfied customer.

And that pleasure is an echo of the pleasure of God when he looked at all he had made and saw it was good.

In the fourth century Christianity became the official religion of the Roman Empire. Very soon it became socially advantageous to go to church. Previously church had been a community of believers – often a persecuted community – in which everyone contributed. Now the church became an institution in which ministry was done by a few. A distinction grew between clergy and laity. Moreover many people were now mere churchgoers. The discipleship of most so-called 'Christians' was notional. So those who wanted to show their dedication to God started going off into the desert to live as hermits or coming together in monastic communities. If you were really keen on following Christ you left the ordinary world and entered the 'religious life'. This, combined with negative Roman attitudes to work, meant the ordinary world of work was undervalued in Christian thinking. Even in monasteries manual work was done by lay people so the monks could be free for the 'spiritual' work of meditation and copying manuscripts.

It didn't help that some people believed the material world was evil. 'Spiritual' became the opposite of 'physical'. Salvation was seen as an escape from the physical body through enlightenment – through the special mystical knowledge of the spiritually élite. This kind of thinking is still with us today. When we hear the word 'spiritual' we don't think of nappies. We think of people kneeling serenely, eyes closed, blocking out the world. When you think of Christian ministry you think of ministers, missionaries, youth leaders and student workers. You don't think of office workers and window cleaners.

It seems that Timothy was encountering an early form of this teaching. Paul tells him to have nothing to do with it (1 Timothy 6:20–21). In 1 Timothy 3:16 Paul talks about 'the *mystery of godliness'*. It's probably a catch phrase of the people causing problems for Timothy. Paul takes their terminology, but gives it a gospel makeover: *'Beyond all question, the mystery of godliness is great: He appeared in a body, was vindicated by the Spirit, was seen by angels, was preached among the nations, was believed on in the world, was taken up in glory'* (1 Timothy 3:16). Jesus appeared 'in a body' so the physical world is sanctified by Jesus. He did the Father's work in a body, not by escaping it. And Jesus is 'taken up in glory' or glorified as he is believed on 'in the world'. You don't see the glory of Jesus in a retreat, but 'in the world'.

Paul goes on to warn Timothy of false teachers who *'forbid people to marry and order them to abstain from certain foods'* (1 Timothy 4:1–3). Paul calls this teaching demonic. You are spiritual, these false teachers argued, by denying your physical appetites for food and sex. The result, however, is that Christians are separated from God (because they spurn his goodness), from other Christians (because they are being élitist) and from the world (because they think they must withdraw). In fact food and sex are good, argues Paul. *'For everything God created is good, and nothing is to be rejected if it is received with thanksgiving, because it is consecrated by the word of God and prayer'* (1 Timothy 4:4–5). 'Consecrated by the word of God and prayer' simply reiterates the previous sentence: we accept that God's word declares creation good and we give thanks to God in prayer.

In 1 Timothy 2:15 Paul says: *'Women will be saved through childbearing – if they continue in faith, love and holiness with propriety.'* The New Living Translation captures the sense well with its footnote: *'by accepting their role as mothers'*. It is a reference to perseverance in the faith. Salvation, for Paul, does not depend from a human point of view on a decision taken long ago, but on perseverance – an ongoing commitment to the Saviour. And that means obedience to Christ in the life-situation in which we find ourselves. The second half of the verse is crucial. Women will be saved through childbearing if they do so with *'faith, love and holiness with propriety'* (2:15). There is a strong parallel with Paul's words to Timothy in chapter 4: *'Watch your life and doctrine closely. Persevere in them, because if you do, you will save both yourself and your hearers'* (4:16). For mothers persevering to the end means being a faithful mother. For Timothy it means being a faithful teacher and leader in the church.

We need to understand 2:15 in the light of Paul's condemnation of 'the doctrine of demons' (4:1–5) (see Fee, 1995). The path to holiness and service, the false teachers argued, was away from the mundane duties of motherhood. They offered more apparently 'spiritual' ministries. But Paul says that holiness and salvation are found not in turning away from marriage and motherhood, but in being a faithful mother. Of course not every Christian woman will be a mother. Paul picks out motherhood not because it's the only way, but because some people were leaving the role of motherhood for more 'glamorous' ministries. And what is true for mothers is true for all Christians. The path of Christian discipleship is not away from the world. We can serve God as we change nappies, write emails, lay bricks, spread plaster, research essays and so on. If we do these things *'in faith, love and holiness with propriety'* we will persevere in our salvation.

So, we should take delight in our work just as God takes delight in his work. But, of course, work is not always the delight God intended! Something has gone wrong.

We can find work frustrating, oppressive and idolatrous

We don't live in the good world that God created. Humanity rejected the rule of God. The Christian understanding of sin shows why work is often frustrating, oppressive and idolatrous.

Work can be frustrating

Sometimes we find great delight in work – that's work as God intended. Work does give people dignity and fulfilment, and bosses should do what they can to ensure work is not demeaning. But often we find work frustrating – that's what work has become as a result of the fall. One consequence of humanity's rebellion against God is that the earth is cursed (Genesis 3:17–19). Work now involves toil and sweat. It becomes frustrating, boring and stressful (Ecclesiastes 2:11, 20–23). Endless emails, projects that go wrong, incompetent management, proposals that come to nothing – these are all part of working in a fallen world.

Work can be oppressive

The frustrating nature of work in a fallen world is compounded by our sin and the sin of others. In our working life we come across difficult customers, conflict with colleagues, workplace bullies. The work environment is not always a happy one. It makes the workplace a tough place to be a Christian. My friend Rob again: 'People get onto dirty jokes, sexist comments, assumptions of dishonesty or impropriety very early in a relationship at work. And if you don't play along you will have to do so publicly. It can be near impossible. The skills needed are tough, and the spiritual support, encouragement and exhortation to persevere are desperately needed.'

The Bible acknowledges that poverty can be caused by laziness (Proverbs 6:6–11; 24:30–34), but more often the Bible portrays injustice and oppression as the root causes of poverty. Proverbs describes the good world that God created as a world of predictable cause and effect in which hard work is rewarded. '*He who works his land will have abundant food, but he who chases fantasies lacks judgment*' (12:11). But now the world is also corrupted by our rebellion. And that means cause and effect doesn't always operate as God intended. Instead, the powerful use their position to exploit the poor. The labour of the marginalized is often exploited. '*A poor man's field may produce abundant food, but injustice sweeps it away*' (Proverbs 13:23). So work can be oppressive.

Work can be idolatrous

The prophet Isaiah condemns the trade of Tyre not only because it exploits, but also because the people of Tyre have used their trade to bring glory to themselves instead of God (Isaiah 23:1–14). The climax of creation is not a person made to work, but a Sabbath made for the glory of God. Henri Blocher (1984) says the Sabbath 'relativizes the works of mankind, the contents of the six working days. It protects mankind from total absorption by the task of subduing the earth, it anticipates the distortion which makes work the sum and purpose of human life.'

Christians find a renewed commitment to working for the glory of God

Humanity was made to live and work for God's glory – that, according to the Westminster Catechisms, is the chief end of man. We forsook that calling when we rebelled against God. But God has redeemed us that we might once again belong to him and seek his glory. The Christian understanding of redemption means we should find a renewed commitment to work through the rediscovery that work can be done for the glory of God.

Slaves, obey your earthly masters in everything; and do it, not only when their eye is on you and to win their favour, but with sincerity of heart and reverence for the Lord. Whatever you do, work at it with all your heart, as working for the Lord, not for men, since you know that you will receive an inheritance from the Lord as a reward. It is the Lord Christ you are serving (Colossians 3:22–24).

We work 'with sincerity of heart and reverence for the Lord'. We work 'as working for the Lord'. We look to 'a reward' from him. 'It is the Lord Christ we are serving'. We should work as if God is our boss – because he is! Paul doesn't simply say we can take delight in our work. We take delight in the fact that *God* takes delight in our work. Even when no-one else recognizes what we do, we can find pleasure in knowing that we are pleasing God. Tim Vickers, who prepares graduates for the transition to work, says: 'The key distinguishing factor will not necessarily be the quality of our work but the motivation of our work . . . It doesn't matter whether our life is wheels or deals, laptops or countertops, or just plain relentless grind . . . our whole life, including our work, matters to God because his glory is at stake in our daily lived-out testimony to him' (Vickers, 2004).

The attitudes of Christians to their work, and their conduct at work, are to commend the gospel. In the good world that God made, taking delight in work and serving others would be its own justification. It would be enough to have done these things in a working day. But the world is no longer like that. Now it is populated with people who are alienated from God; people who need to hear the good news. And so the workplace has also become an important place to witness to Christ through word and deed. We worry about how we can build gospel relationships in our neighbourhood, but at work those relationships already exist. Unbelievers can throw away a gospel tract, send away the person who knocks on the door, turn off *Songs of Praise*. But they can't avoid the gospel witness of a Christian colleague. 'Often the people who know us well don't live next door, they work at the next desk,' says Mark Greene. 'We fish in pools and puddles when in our workplace we are sitting by an ocean' (Greene, 2005). One friend wrote to me: 'We need to recognize the profoundness of work relationships. My colleagues are far more likely to see me in a high stress situation than my family, friends or contacts out of work. It must create opportunities for real friendship and gospel opportunity. Colleagues see deep things about each other.' Paul recognized the huge potential of the workplace for evangelism:

> Make it your ambition to lead a quiet life, to mind your own business and to work with your hands, just as we told you, so that your daily life may win the respect of outsiders and so that you will not be dependent on anybody (1 Thessalonians 4:11–12).

> Teach slaves to be subject to their masters in everything, to try to please them, not to talk back to them, and not to steal from them, but to show that they can be fully trusted, so that in every way they will make the teaching about God our Saviour attractive (Titus 2:9–10).

Opportunities to follow up the witness of work often take place off-site and out of work hours. You may get a chance to say something in a tea break, but the opportunity to talk in depth is more likely to come in the pub after work. And that means as churches we need to recognize and value these opportunities even if it means Christians can't always get to church activities as a result. The important thing is the intention. You can't say, 'I don't have time for church activities because work is my ministry' unless you intentionally and deliberately make work a feature of your ministry. We need to approach each day as ministry – serving others and looking for opportunities to share the gospel. As one teacher said to me, 'I always pray before I lead a Bible study, so why not before I take a lesson?' We need to approach our work in just the same way as we approach other ministry activities.

In the new creation we will delight in glorifying God through work and service

Work in a fallen world can be frustrating and oppressive. But Isaiah looks forward to a day when people will enjoy the fruit of their labour as God intended: *'my chosen ones will long enjoy the works of their hands'* (Isaiah 65:21–22). Although Isaiah announces the fall of the idolatrous trading empire of Tyre, he also speaks of her restoration. Once again she will *'ply her trade with all the kingdoms on the face of the earth'*. This time *'her profit and her earnings will be set apart for the LORD'* (23:17–18). He looks forward to a day when the trading wealth of the nations will be used not for selfish, proud human ends, but for the glory of God and the provision of his people (Isaiah 60:5; Revelation 21:24–26). Paul implies that the redemption of humanity will lead to the lifting of the curse over creation (Romans 8:19–21). We will be restored to our role as God's co-workers, ruling over, and caring for, creation. And through our redeemed labour creation itself will also be redeemed. John says that God's redeemed people will serve him, but without the threat of poverty or the heat of toil (Revelation 7:13–17).

But we are not yet there. Some Christians I talk to seem to think they have the right to a job that is constantly pleasant and fulfilling. They become indignant when life isn't like that. They're like Christians who expect God to make them healthy all the time. We live in a fallen world that is not yet redeemed. So don't be surprised if work is often boring or frustrating. Set your sights on the new creation when work will be a delight.

Getting God to work

For many Christians 'church' has become another pressure in their overburdened lives. One friend wrote to me: 'Growing up in south Wales, we had a 10.30 morning service, my mother taught a Sunday school class at two, my father taught a class at three, and we were back at church for the evening service! A Sabbath rest? No, another busy day.' Many of my friends enjoy their house groups, but dread the early evening rush to cook, eat and deal with children first.

Part of the problem is that many of us see our commitments to work, family and church in tension and competition. Doing more mission means squeezing time for something else.

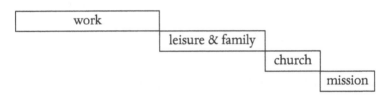

Western culture has become very compartmentalized. The public world of work and the private world of home have their own codes of conduct. Faith is acceptable at home, but isn't supposed to intrude into the public world of business, education or politics. You might pray with your family before a meal, but you don't pray before a work meeting. My friend was converted at the very end of his time at school. He happened to be going away for the summer so it was a few weeks before he first attended church. When he did so he thought revival had happened because many of his school friends were there. In fact, they'd always gone to church, but he'd never known. His friends lived different lives in different circles. We need to make our circles overlap. We need to make church and mission part of our very identity instead of add-on activities. (For more on private faith and public work, see Chester, 2004.)

And that means rethinking evangelism as relationships rather than events and rethinking church as a community rather than an organization. Relationships are the fabric of church and mission. Ordinary life becomes pastoral and missional if we have 'gospel intentionality'. If mission and church are redefined in relational terms and we do everything in the light of our commitment to the gospel, then work, leisure and family time can all be viewed as gospel activities.

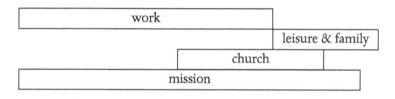

Recently a Christian friend came to visit for the weekend. He supports West Ham so we went to Bramall Lane to see them play Sheffield United. I also took my daughter Katie and an unbelieving friend from Thailand. Afterwards the Thai woman came back to our house for a meal. Is that leisure and family time? Yes. But it was also mission and church. A similar thing had happened the week before. We went for a walk with another family from our church plus a couple of single people and one of their unbelieving friends. Was that family time or leisure time or church time or mission time? It was all of them.

The book of Zechariah ends with a vision of a day when even cooking pots will be inscribed 'HOLY TO THE LORD' (Zechariah 14:20–21). That day is the coming of Jesus. Now the ordinary can be holy to God. We can even offer up our washing up as a holy act, consecrated to God's glory. What difference would it make if 'HOLY TO THE LORD' were written on your worktop, computer or car dashboard? Why not write 'HOLY TO THE LORD' on a sticker and put it in a prominent position?

6. GETTING TO THE HEART OF BUSYNESS

How much extra time each day do you need to complete all you need or want to do? Thirty minutes? An hour? Two hours? Or would you prefer an extra day a week? Terry Pratchett has a story called *Thief of Time* in which time is managed by 'the Monks of History'. The Monks can store time and pump it around. They take it from places where it's not needed like under water or high up on mountains (how much time does a stone need?). Then they pump it to cities where there's never enough time. Do you wish some sort of system like that operated in reality?

It seems that God made a mistake when he first spun the world into space. That initial twist with his fingers that set the earth revolving was just a bit too energetic. And so now the earth spins round once every 24 hours. If only God had spun it a little slower we would have had 25 or 26 hours in the day. Then we'd have time enough for everything. Just think what you could do with that extra hour: get on top of your work, read with your children, complete some further study, have a regular quiet time. If only.

Doing more than God expects

But of course God doesn't make mistakes. Twenty-four-hour days were part of the world God declared very good. The problem is not that there isn't enough time for what we want to do. The problem is we're trying to do too much. We haven't come to terms with the fact that we are finite and limited.

People do *not* feel stressed simply because they have a lot on. Most of us enjoy doing lots of things. We only feel busy when we try to do *more than we can*. The problem is not expecting to do a lot, but expecting that little bit more than is possible. In Charles Dickens's novel *David Copperfield*, Mr Micawber famously gives the following advice: 'Annual income twenty pounds, annual expenditure nineteen nineteen six, result happiness. Annual income twenty pounds, annual expenditure twenty pounds ought and six, result misery.' So it is with time. If we're doing a lot, but can cope, then we are content in our busyness. But what happens when we find ourselves trying to do more than we can? We not only get stressed about the extra demands that have tipped us over. We feel stressed about *everything* we have to do. I remember talking to a young woman who felt her whole life was full of stress. 'I feel like running away,' she told me. Other people looking on might have wondered what the problem was. Her life wasn't crammed with activities. But it only took a few things beyond what she could cope with to make her feel everything was impossible.

So here's a foundational truth for what follows: *God does not expect me to do more than I can.*

Stated like that, it's obvious. Clearly God doesn't expect me to work twenty-six hours a day or eight days a week. In fact he doesn't even expect me to work seven days a week, for the Bible commends a day of rest. We need to learn that we have limitations and not to be afraid to admit these to ourselves or others. Some of these limitations are to do with time, others are to do with our physical and emotional capacity. Until my mid-thirties the main constraint on my activities was lack of time – a deficiency I solved every now and then with a series of late nights. Now my main limitation is energy – and late nights only make it worse! When pushed beyond these limits, we often transfer our stresses and frustrations to others. We accuse our boss or church leaders of making us work too hard, but still say 'Yes' when they ask us to do something new. Many of us fail to say 'No' and then compensate by bearing grudges, complaining or doing a bad job.

If God doesn't expect me to do more than I can, the key question to ask ourselves is: *Why I am trying to do more than I can?*

We've seen how prevalent the problem of busyness is in our society and our own lives. We've seen that God made us so that we would work hard and be fruitful, but also to rest and play. Somehow we've got our lives out of kilter. If you've been in the workplace for any length of time you'll probably have come across much of the time management advice in the previous chapters. The very fact that you're reading this book suggests that it has not entirely worked for you. Resolutions to manage time better, to get our 'work–life balance' sorted, to find more time for rest and service, don't seem to get us very far. Like most New Year resolutions, they don't last much beyond the first week of January. The reason is that what drives our busyness is not simply our inability to use time efficiently or sort out our priorities. If we are going to tackle the problem of busyness we need to tackle the pressures that drive it. We need to explore *why* we are so busy.

Take your time

'Slow down, you move too fast, you've got to make the morning last,' sang Paul Simon. So many things can be a pleasure if you take your time. Consider a visit to the shops. We're so conditioned to rush that every stage is fraught with tension. We drive as fast as we can, get impatient at traffic lights, take every opportunity to overtake. We're disappointed if we can't park near the entrance, and once inside we're frustrated by slow trolleys and slow trolley drivers. We get cross about long checkout queues and slow checkout assistants. The whole experience is a strain. And what have we gained? A couple of minutes at the most – plus an ulcer. Most of the time, if you exceed the speed limit you only end up waiting longer at the next set of traffic lights. But what if you take your time, laugh at other frenetic drivers busy going nowhere, give way to irate trolley drivers, talk to other customers? Or what if you walk to your local shops, chat to shop staff, admire other people's gardens, listen out for birdsong, take a detour through the park? You may lose a few minutes from your schedule, but you will gain half an hour of pleasure. You know it makes sense! But we don't do it because deep in our hearts we are wired for speed. We are driven people.

Busy hearts

Over some pressures we have only limited control. On our own, few of us can change the culture of our workplace. Some people in low-paid jobs are forced by economic necessity to work long hours. Parents of young children live life in a blur for a few years. Evangelical Christians were involved in nineteenth-century efforts to reduce working hours and improve working conditions, and evangelicals today need to engage with our contemporary corporate culture.

But I want to suggest that much, perhaps most, of the pressure to be busy comes from within. Oswald Sanders (1958) says: 'Work, even hard work, when the mind is at rest, is health giving. It produces fatigue but no tension. The fundamental cause of strain is to be found in the mind, not in the body.' There was a period in my life when I combined a full-time job with two hours a day on a PhD, weekly preaching and raising two pre-school children. I would get physically tired, but I had no complaints – I loved it all and found it energizing. At other times I've hardly done one useful thing all day. I've been listless, restless and weary.

At the heart of our busyness is our heart. We're busy because we're working hard to meet the desires of our hearts. Does that mean I'm busy because I want to be? Yes and no. No, in the sense that you don't specifically choose to be overworked, stressed and run down. Yes, in the sense that your busyness is the result of the choices you make. It's a product of the desires of your heart – and not all those desires are godly!

In Romans 1:24–25 Paul says of humanity: '*God gave them over in the sinful desires of their hearts to sexual impurity for the degrading of their bodies with one another. They exchanged the truth of God for a lie, and worshipped and served created things rather than the Creator – who is for ever praised. Amen.*' Notice how impure behaviour arises from the sinful desires of our hearts. Paul gives a long list of such behaviour in verses 29–31, but it all comes from the heart. But notice, too, that the sinful desires of our hearts arise because we have exchanged the truth about God for a lie and worshipped the creature rather than the Creator. In other words, *our thoughts and desires are the source of our behaviour and emotions.* The Bible connects all these with what it calls our 'heart' – our inner self. Jesus says: '*For from within, out of men's hearts, come evil thoughts, sexual immorality, theft, murder, adultery, greed, malice, deceit, lewdness, envy, slander, arrogance and folly'* (Mark 7:21–22). Behind every sin is a lie. Sin arises when we believe lies about God and about ourselves. The thinking of our hearts and the desires of our hearts shape the choices of our hearts (our will). This is true of both our good behaviour and our sinful behaviour. One arises from good desires informed by truth; the other from evil desires shaped by lies or a desire for good things that has grown bigger than God. Submission to God, faith in the truth and a heart set on God lead to godly behaviour and emotions. Idolatry, unbelief and sinful desires lead to sinful behaviour and negative emotions.

Madeline Bunting (2004) calls her book on overwork, *Willing Slaves*. It's actually a good description of sinners. We choose to live without God and suppress the truth by our wickedness (Romans 1:18). We exchange the truth of God for a lie and worship created things rather than the Creator (Romans 1:25). But the gods we create become our masters. We are enslaved by them. They genuinely control us unless and until we return to the truth about God. We become trapped in harmful patterns of behaviour. We become 'willing slaves'. This is true of our busyness. We feel trapped in our busyness. Our lives feel out of control. And indeed they are. But God can set us free – not by rearranging our schedule, but by liberating us from the lies and evil desires that control us.

We often claim that our behaviour and emotions are the result of external pressures. We might say, for example, 'I lost my temper because I was provoked' or 'I feel depressed because of all I've been through'. External pressures *are* significant, but they only lead to sin because of our sinful desires (see James 1:13–15). In other words, external pressures impact on our behaviour *via our hearts*. Suppose I get angry because someone smashes my car. If my car had not been smashed I would not have got angry. But having my car smashed doesn't fully explain my anger. My anger came from my heart. It was a sinful response from a sinful heart (James 4:1–2). It revealed my idolatry (my love of my car or myself or my need to be in control). The heart is *deceitful above all things* (Jeremiah 17:9; see also Ephesians 4:22; Titus 3:3; Hebrews 3:13). Our sinful hearts delude us. They persuade us that our actions are inevitable, unavoidable or appropriate. If someone smashes my car, I assume my anger is inevitable, unavoidable and appropriate. But the truth is that it reveals my idolatry.

Do you ever think your busyness is inevitable, unavoidable or appropriate? I want to suggest that it may be none of those things.

Think about what that might mean for your busyness. Do you ever think your busyness is inevitable, unavoidable or appropriate? I want to suggest that it may be none of those things. It may be that your heart is deceiving you. I once met a young boy in India. I guess he was about seven or eight. He worked 14 hours a day picking over the local rubbish dump for anything that could be sold for recycling. I also met bonded labourers, forced to break rocks in the heat of the sun to repay debts over years, in some cases over generations. They had no choice about their 'busyness'. *But you do.*

I once asked the founder and CEO of a multinational company if people really could work fewer hours? Would it be possible? His unequivocal answer was 'Yes'. If, say, the Prime Minister wanted to work a 50-hour week, he could do so. He would need to delegate more and decide what was important for him to focus on, but it could be done. He pointed out that we have employment legislation that protects workers. People don't have to work longer than their contracted hours. The European Union Working Time Directive means you can't be forced to work more than 48 hours a week. People talk of 'presenteeism' – the practice of staying on at work to impress, or meet expectations, even when there's little to do that's genuinely productive. A few people are what are sometimes called 'wage slaves' – people forced by economic necessity to work long hours. But most of us think of ourselves as slaves to work when in reality we are slaves to our own sinful desires. We have suggested that step one in addressing busyness is *to use your time efficiently*, step two is *to sort out your priorities* and step three is *to glorify God all the time*. But the most important step is step four: *Identify the desires of your heart that make you try to do more than God expects of you.*

Another word the Bible uses to talk about the sinful desires of our hearts is 'the flesh' or 'the lusts of the flesh' ('lust' here doesn't simply mean sexual desire, but any wrong desire). The flesh has two other companions: the world and the devil. In Ephesians 2:1–3 Paul says Christians used to follow:

- the ways of this world
- the ways of the ruler of the kingdom of the air = Satan
- the sinful nature (literally 'the lusts of the flesh')

Sadly, as Ephesians 6 makes clear, this struggle with the world, the flesh and the devil didn't end when we became Christians. The lies that shape the desires of our hearts that lead to our over-busy lives are lies promoted by Satan through the world around us that resonate with our sinful hearts. Satan is the father of lies. That's how he operates. In the Garden of Eden God ruled his people. His rule was a rule of joy, peace, blessing and freedom. And he ruled through his word – through the word that brought creation into being, expressed in the command not to eat from the tree of the knowledge of good and evil. When the serpent came to Eve he caused her to doubt God's word (*'Did God really say . . .?'*, Genesis 3:1) and question God's rule (*'you will be like God'*, Genesis 3:5). He portrayed God's rule as tyrannical. He promised Eve freedom, but we ended up enslaved to sin and death. God rules through his word. Satan rules through his lies. God's rule brings freedom. Satan's rule brings slavery.

Listen to the words of Jesus. They'll help you spot whether your busyness is idolatrous or not.

> *No good tree bears bad fruit, nor does a bad tree bear good fruit. Each tree is recognised by its own fruit. People do not pick figs from thorn-bushes, or grapes from briars. The good man brings good things out of the good stored up in his heart, and the evil man brings evil things out of the evil stored up in his heart. For out of the overflow of his heart his mouth speaks* (Luke 6:43–45).

The test you need to apply to your busyness is this: if it produces bad fruit then it reflects the evil desires of your heart. *We can spot idolatrous busyness because it will eventually cause harm – in our bodies, our families, our churches and our relationship with God.* If your health, marriage, friendships, Christian service or relationship with God is suffering because of your busyness then you need to address the idols in your life. You need to *identify the desires of your heart that make you try to do more than God expects of you.*

To help identify these heart desires, think about why you say 'Yes' to requests when you want to say 'No':

- Because I need to prove myself . . . work gives me a sense of identity, meaning and purpose . . . I feel good

about myself when I'm busy . . . I need to justify myself
to others . . .
- Because of other people's expectations . . . I don't want
  to let others down . . . I want to get it right . . .
- Because otherwise things get out of control . . . I'm
  worried about my job, my future, my security . . . other
  people need me . . .
- Because I prefer the pressure . . . I've got a deadline
  looming . . . I leave things to the last moment . . . I find
  it easier to be busy . . .
- Because I need the money . . . I'm working to pay off
  my debts . . . there are things I need to buy . . .
- Because I want to make the most of life . . . there are
  things I want to achieve at work . . . there are places I
  want to visit . . . skills I want to master . . . things I want
  to do . . .

'There is a way that seems right to a man, but in the end it leads
to death' (Proverbs 14:12). All these statements seem right to
us. They make perfect sense, especially since they're re-
inforced by our culture. But they lead to deadly, life-defeating
weariness. If you still find it hard to believe that you collude
in your own busyness then stick with me for the next few
chapters. 'All a man's ways seem innocent to him, but motives are
weighed by the LORD' (Proverbs 16:2). Invite God to examine the
motives of your heart as you read. Everyone is different. We
are susceptible to different pressures and temptations. But
some of what I say may resonate with your experience.

There are solutions. But they are not instant solutions. It
takes time to change habits of thought and the desires of our
hearts. Indeed it's a lifelong task. We need repeatedly to speak
the truth about God to ourselves. We need other people who
will remind of us of that truth often; people who love us

enough to call us to repent of our idols and sinful desires. We need to make the links between our behaviour and the thinking and desires that underlie that behaviour. The ability to make those links is what the Bible calls wisdom, and James invites those who lack wisdom to pray for it (James 1:5).

I want to identify some of the lies promoted by the world and the devil that lead people to be over-busy. In each case we will also explore the counter-truth – the liberating promises of God. I remember being in a prayer meeting when Mrs Perry, a wonderful, godly lady in our church, told us that it was the seventieth anniversary of her baptism. It was so moving to think of this daughter of God having walked with him and been kept by him for seventy years. Mrs Perry once passed on this quote to my father:

> Rest for the mind in his word.
> Rest for the conscience in his blood.
> Rest for the heart in his care.

If you want rest from your busyness then listen to Mrs Perry. Then you too might be able to stay the course and run the Christian race for seventy years.

Our struggle with busyness is the struggle to believe God's liberating promises for ourselves so that they shape our attitudes and actions. We may feel enslaved by our busyness and our schedules. But at the root of that slavery are the lies of Satan which are perpetrated by our culture. If we are to be set free, we must expose those lies and counter them with God's word. More important than managing time is managing our hearts.

7. I'M BUSY BECAUSE I NEED TO PROVE MYSELF – *THE LIBERATING REST OF GOD*

'So what can I do about my busyness?' Perhaps that's what you hoped this book would tell you. But the question itself is flawed. What if I told you five things you could do about your busyness? Where would that leave you? With five extra things to fit into your schedule, you'd be busier than ever! Busyness is one problem we can't solve by doing more! But the situation is not hopeless. We're not doomed to be busy. Someone *has* done something about our busyness – the Lord Jesus Christ. You don't need to 'do' more to overcome busyness because Jesus has already done all that is required. 'It is finished!' he cried. 'The job is done. The work is complete.' The key is to see the link between Christ's finished work and our never-ending busyness.

The rest of grace
Jesus said: '*Come to me, all you who are weary and burdened, and I will give you rest. Take my yoke upon you and learn from me, for I am*

gentle and humble in heart, and you will find rest for your souls. For my yoke is easy and my burden is light' (Matthew 11:28–30). The preceding verses describe how the religious and privileged people reject Jesus (verses 11–24). *'At that time Jesus said, "I praise you, Father, Lord of heaven and earth, because you have hidden these things from the wise and learned, and revealed them to little children. Yes, Father, for this was your good pleasure"'* (verses 25–26). The Father reveals the truth to the humble and lowly, and hides it from the proud and self-important. That is the wonder of grace. Salvation doesn't depend on status, intellect or wealth; nor on activity or achievement. It depends solely on the sovereign grace of God. And, as if to demonstrate that, God delights to choose 'little children' (see also 1 Corinthians 1:26–31). The Son reveals the truth to those whom he chooses (verse 27).

The revelation of the Son comes in the invitation to find rest. Here is this invitation of grace. And we don't come with our wisdom or status, our achievement or activities. We bring our weariness and burdens. The Rabbis spoke of 'the yoke of the law'. You made yourself right with God through obedience to the law – plus all the regulations the Pharisees had added. The contrast in Jesus' invitation is not between work and rest. It's between justification by works and justification by grace. The Pharisees wanted to prove themselves right with God through their religious works. But Jesus says that is a wearying burden that ends in oppression. Instead, he offers justification by grace that leads to freedom and rest. Observance of Sabbath rest was *'a sign between me and you for the generations to come, so that you may know that I am the LORD, who makes you holy'* (Exodus 31:13). Sabbath was a reminder that it is God who makes us holy. We are saved because of the choice of the Father and the Son (verses 25–27). We contribute nothing to that choice. We don't have to prove ourselves to God.

The lie: justification by work

Today we have a secular version of justification by works. In the medieval worldview a person was justified before God through religious works. So the path of spirituality lay in contemplation and detachment from the everyday world. The Reformation was the rediscovery of justification by grace. It undermined attempts to justify oneself through religion. Christian discipleship was expressed through faithfulness to God in everyday activities. People often talk about the 'Protestant work ethic'. The Protestant work ethic is the commitment to work that arose because of the value given to all of life by the Reformation.

Today the Protestant work ethic is often said to be the underlying cause of the stress-filled world of modern work. As we become a culture of workaholics, Christianity is blamed. But the problem is not the Protestant work ethic, but the secularized work ethic of the Enlightenment.

In Reformation teaching, work was one of the ways by which you glorified God and served other people. Rest was another way you glorified God. It was God who gave work its value. God was ultimate and work was penultimate. You found meaning and identity through serving God. But what happened with secularization was that God was taken out of the equation (for more on the secularized work ethic, see Ryken, 1989). Now you found meaning through work itself. Your sense of being a person of worth was found not through your relationship to God but through work itself. People started to justify themselves through their secular jobs or roles. People often associate the Protestant work ethic with a 'pull yourself up by your boot-straps' self-reliance. 'In fact,' comments Alister McGrath (1991), 'this amounts to a serious misunderstanding of the original Reformation work ethic. The Reformers continually stressed that we are what we are by the grace of God, not by dint of human effort. The notion of an achievement-centred spirituality was alien to the reformers, who mounted a sustained and radical critique of the theological foundations of the idea.'

So today people find identity through work itself. We answer the question, 'What do you do?' with a job title. We answer the question, 'What are you worth?' with a salary figure. Robert Banks (1983) concludes: 'The pressure of time in everyday life is not primarily the result of the development or distribution of clocks and watches. More significant were changes in worldview leading to a less God-centred and grace-based approach to life in favour of a more man-centred and work-justifying attitude.' This creates the drive to work and work and work. Your identity depends on it. And so we work on, even though it is harming our health, our families and our relationships. 'We don't want to rest because we want to be indispensable. We don't want to stop being productive because our identities are rooted in activity and accomplishment' (Baab, 2005).

This is what makes unemployment or retirement so devastating to some people. When work is taken away their identity is taken away. The demon-possessed man from the Gerasenes who was set free by Jesus was at it *night and day* (Mark 5:5). And there is a demonic frenzy about life today.

> *We're busy, busy, busy because we're trying to serve a god who cannot be placated.*

We're busy, busy, busy because we're trying to serve a god who cannot be placated. We're pursing fulfilment in what cannot fulfil. Research by the Work Foundation found that, contrary to expectations, close supervision reduces working hours. It is those who are less supervised who feel compelled to work long hours. It is driven by self-justification. Beverley Shepherd (2003) says: 'The attempt to justify our existence and prove our acceptability through achievement and activity . . . leads to an unending cycle of grief – unending because no achievement or amount of activity can fully satisfy our need for acceptance . . . We may talk about wanting to get off the bullet train of Western society, but the reality is that we are afraid – afraid of being a nobody.'

The information revolution accentuates the drive for justification by work. It offers greater potential for 'self-actualization' through work. More workers than ever in post-industrial societies are doing jobs that are intrinsically fulfilling. We're no longer cogs in the machine or units in the production process. We have opportunities for creativity and initiative. This is a great blessing. But it also tempts us to find identity and value through 'rewarding' work. In the Reformation all work was seen as intrinsically good as long as it was moral. The value of work was measured by the glory it brought to God and the service it rendered to others. A road sweeper could take pride in the clean streets he provided for the community. But in the information age, the value of work is measured by the sense of self-fulfilment it brings. Work is judged not by the service it renders to others, but by the service it renders to me, the worker.

Sociologist Zygmunt Bauman (1998) says the trick today is not to limit work time to create leisure time, but to remove the line between work and recreation; to 'lift work itself to the rank of supreme and most satisfying entertainment'. Such a job is highly coveted and much sought after. 'Work that is rich in gratifying experience, work as self-fulfilment, work as the meaning of life, work as the core or the axis of everything that counts, as the source of pride, self-esteem,

honour and deference or notoriety, in short as vocation has
become the privilege of the few, a distinctive mark of the
élite, a way of life the rest may watch in awe, admire and con-
template at a distance.' In other words, work has become a
god. Reread the quote replacing the word 'work' with 'God':
'. . . God is the meaning of life, God is the core or the axis of
everything that counts, the source of pride . . .' The élite find
salvation (meaning fulfilment and honour) through 'rewarding' jobs. The rest work all the harder to achieve this secular
salvation.

Meaning-through-work is well suited to the goals of business. Management gurus like Tom Peters and Charles Handy
have argued (2004) that 'a huge reserve of energy and commitment could be tapped by a corporation which offers its
management a chance to make . . . not just money, but *meaning
for people*'. As Peters puts it in his book *In Search of Excellence*:
'We desperately need meaning in our lives and will sacrifice a
great deal to institutions that will provide meaning for us'
(Bunting, 2004). An endless stream of management books,
tapes and courses no longer content themselves with telling us
how to chair a good meeting or make a good product. Now
they promise to release your inner potential so you can find
meaning and fulfilment. They offer salvation from within.
'This goes a long way to explaining,' comments Madeleine
Bunting, 'why the harried senior executive willingly forgoes
the freedom of his own time, and accepts the trade-off of inva-
sive work for the pleasures of being needed, and involved in
something meaningful' (Bunting, 2004). Corporations speak
in quasi-religious language of identity, meaning, mission and
values. They are in the business of capturing hearts and minds.
They even speak the language of love: in our culture the language of 'passion' belongs as much in the boardroom as in the
bedroom. Bunting says this:

A work ethic has evolved that promotes a particular sense of self
and identity which meshes neatly with the needs of market
capitalism, through consumption and through work. Put at its
simplest, narcissism and capitalism are mutually reinforcing.
What is pushed to the margin are the time-consuming, labour-
intensive human relationships, and doing nothing – simply being.
Clever organizations exploit this cultural context, this craving for
control, self-assertion and self-affirmation, and design corporate
cultures which meet the emotional needs of their employees
(Bunting, 2004).

We have made work an idol for workers, offering salvation
(identity and fulfilment) through work and we have made consumption an idol for consumers, offering salvation through
shopping. Bunting (2004) adds: 'The cleverness of the fit
between the project of the self and this work ethic is that it is
self-reinforcing. There is no resting point: the project of the
self is never complete, and is always riddled with anxiety and
insecurities.' 'There is no resting point.' That's because neither
work nor consumption can give salvation. 'The project of the
self' is an idolatrous project and idols never satisfy. The secret
is to call time on the 'project of the self' and turn back to God.
This is what the Bible calls repentance. 'There is no resting
point' for those seeking salvation through work. But Jesus
says: 'Come to me and I will give you rest.'

One senior pastor described to me how people say to him:
'We didn't trouble you because we know how busy you are.'
He realized they were in effect saying: 'You're important so
you must be busy.' Busyness is a sign of virtue and value.
Busyness is next to godliness. A friend in his early forties
asked me recently: 'Why are so many twenty-year-olds tired
all the time?' The answer may be that they live in a culture of
tiredness in which people think being tired is inevitable and

normal. Our grandparents saw leisure as a sign of status. But now overwork is a sign of status. The constant interruptions of mobile phones, the presence of business papers on the train, the laptop on holiday – all make us feel important and valuable. Young people really do feel tired, but often it's self-generated, maybe even psychosomatic, because if you're not tired then you're not worthwhile.

The attempt to justify or prove ourselves through busyness is prevalent not only in secular work, but also in Christian ministry. A friend of mine used to be on the management team of a large Christian organization. As part of his role he got to see the time sheets of the workers. Some staff, he noted, worked as many as twice the hours that others worked. But instead of commending the 'godliness' of the over-workers, he noted that they were the most insecure people within the organization. They overworked because they felt they needed to prove themselves. An evangelist said to me: '"I'm really busy" is a phrase I hear a lot from Christians. It annoys me. I used to say it myself because I wanted people to think I was busy. It makes you look good. It makes you feel like you're a worthy Christian, that people will admire you.'

Pastors preach justification by faith and then tell you at the door how busy they are, in an act of hypocritical self-justification. On the first ever management training course I attended we were given some advice which I've always remembered: Don't tell people you are busy. If you tell people you're busy what they will hear is, 'I don't have time for you.' It's advice I've tried to carry over into pastoral ministry. Yet the temptation to talk up our busyness is strong. We want to show we're earning our money. We want people to respect our hard work. But all the time we are making people reluctant to approach us. This is true in business, the church and families. Our desire to justify ourselves means that problems go unaddressed.

The truth: justification by grace

There's nothing wrong with being busy. Most of us enjoy being busy. What creates stress is the feeling that we cannot meet the expectations of others or of God. But Jesus offers rest from the burden of self-justification. We are accepted by God. This is how we find meaning and value. At the most fundamental level, Tim Chester is a justified sinner. I'm not fundamentally a writer, or preacher, or even a husband and father. I am a sinner saved by grace and all I contribute to that identity is the sin bit. I don't need to prove myself as a sinner saved by grace. Instead I praise the gracious embrace of the Father, the complete atonement of the Son and the Spirit's enabling presence. This is who I am. And it's a gift. I don't need to earn it.

A church member once said to his pastor: 'I phoned you on Monday, but there was no reply.' 'Yes,' replied the pastor, 'Monday is my day off.' 'A day off!' replied the church member with self-righteous indignation. 'The devil doesn't take a day off.' 'That's right,' said the pastor, 'and if I didn't take any time off, I'd be just like him.' The devil cannot rest. Only those justified by grace can truly rest. A youth worker was complaining to me of being tired. It turned out he was getting up at six each morning because it made him feel more holy. 'Isn't the death of Christ enough?' I asked. 'Do you really have to finish off what Christ left undone by getting up early?' In the temple the work of atonement was never done. '*Day after day every priest stands and performs his religious duties; again and again he offers the same sacrifices, which can never take away sins.*' But Jesus '*offered for all time one sacrifice for sins, he sat down at the right hand of God*' (Hebrews 10:11–12). Jesus has sat down. He has done all that is required. So we can sit down as well. We don't have to be up and about trying to make atonement. Bruce Milne (1993) says: 'The Christian is called to affirm the completeness and sufficiency of [Christ's] sacrifice by trusting in it constantly and by exhibiting the peace and confidence which are the fruit of such a trust. Our often strained and frenetic forms of Christian life are witness to how much we need to affirm again with Jesus, "It is accomplished!" *It is finished!'*

A still heart – a meditation on Psalms 130 and 131

Psalm 130

Out of the depths I cry to you, O LORD;

² O Lord, hear my voice.

Let your ears be attentive

to my cry for mercy.

³ If you, O LORD, kept a record of sins,

O Lord, who could stand?

⁴ But with you there is forgiveness;

therefore you are feared.

One might suppose that the LORD could only be addressed by important people living blameless lives. But this is the Psalm of a self-confessed sinner crying out for mercy from the depths. Draw up a mental record of your sins over the last day, week, year. This record means you could never stand before God. But this judgment is overridden in verse 4. There is forgiveness with God. *'If you, O LORD, kept a record of sins . . .'* says verse 3. But verse 4 tells us that God does *not* keep a record of sins. God says: *'I will forgive their wickedness and will remember their sins no more'* (Hebrews 8:12). In this one area alone you have a better memory than God! The sins you think you need to make good, he has forgotten.

> *⁵ I wait for the* LORD, *my soul waits,*
> *and in his word I put my hope.*
> *⁶ My soul waits for the Lord*
> *more than watchmen wait for the morning,*
> *more than watchmen wait for the morning.*

What is the answer to busyness? It is to wait: to wait for the LORD and put our hope in his word. Think of all the ways you are restless trying to prove yourself or establish your identity. Think of the times you are busy to impress others. The Psalmist tells us to stop our frenetic activity and wait for the LORD.

> *⁷ O Israel, put your hope in the* LORD,
> *for with the* LORD *is unfailing love*
> *and with him is full redemption.*
> *⁸ He himself will redeem Israel*
> *from all their sins.*

God himself entered our world to redeem his people from all their sins. He became a man, lived among us, humbled himself and became obedient to death. On the cross he took our place. He was the sacrifice of atonement and the Passover Lamb who redeems God's people. And so with the LORD is *unfailing love* and *full redemption*. Unfailing and complete. His love never runs out and his salvation is wholly adequate. Every act of self-justification is a denial that with the LORD there is full redemption. We act as if Christ's death goes so far, but we somehow need to be busy completing the job with our petty attempts to self-atone. We act as if God's love will fail if we are not busy proving ourselves worthy. Unfailing love and full redemption set us free ('redeem us') from self-justifying busyness.

Psalm 131

*My heart is not proud, O L*ORD*,*
my eyes are not haughty;
I do not concern myself with great matters
or things too wonderful for me.
² But I have stilled and quietened my soul;
like a weaned child with its mother,
like a weaned child is my soul within me.
*³ O Israel, put your hope in the L*ORD
both now and for evermore.

David Powlison (2003) writes: 'This man isn't noisy inside. He isn't busy-busy-busy. Not obsessed or on edge. Pressures to achieve don't consume him. Failure and despair don't haunt him. Anxiety isn't spinning him into freefall. Regrets don't corrode his inner experience. He's not stumbling through the minefield of blind longings and fears. He's quiet.' This is a Psalm 'of David'. Think of everything you know about the life of David. Was it a quiet life? Did he retreat from the world? Was it problem-free? This is a still and quiet heart in the midst of a fraught and busy life.

*¹ My heart is not proud, O L*ORD*,*
my eyes are not haughty;
I do not concern myself with great matters
or things too wonderful for me.

Think of the opposite of verse one: 'My heart wants to be valued, I'm looking for recognition; I'm concerned to be great and do wonderful things.' Powlison (2003) says: 'Your biggest problem is proud self-will. That's the noise-machine inside you.' The desire for recognition, significance, achievement, to be valued and accepted – these are the noises in our hearts. Powlison (2003) asks: 'Are you quiet inside? Is Psalm 131 your experience, too? If your answer is No, what is the "noise" going on inside you? Where does it come from? How do you get busy and preoccupied? Why do you lose your composure? When do you get worried, irritable, wearied, or hopeless? How can you regain composure?'

² But I have stilled and quietened my soul;
like a weaned child with its mother,
like a weaned child is my soul within me.

Imagine a nursing child hungry for its mother's milk. She is grouchy, restless, irritable until she can suckle. One moment she can be chuckling happily on your lap. But once she wants milk, no amount of bouncing, singing or funny faces will calm her. If you try to hold her, she wriggles, cries and squirms. She shows anger, frustration, anxiety and jealousy. But David is like a weaned child who is no longer restless. David has weaned himself off the noises of his heart. He has shushed quiet the desire to justify himself; to control his life; to achieve glory.

³ O Israel, put your hope in the LORD
both now and for evermore.

This is the secret of a still heart. In verse 1 David stopped hoping in himself. Instead he hopes in the LORD now and for ever. Often we can do 'for ever' – we have hope that God will save us on the final day. But what about 'now'? What about tomorrow in your workplace? What about the next time you want to prove yourself? What about when you face the next deadline? What about when you feel you have to make it up to God? Or when someone questions your commitment? Identify now the truths you will cling to in those moments.

8. I'M BUSY BECAUSE OF OTHER PEOPLE'S EXPECTATIONS – *THE LIBERATING FEAR OF GOD*

You're just about to dash off so you can get home for the church prayer meeting when your boss comes over to your desk: 'Can you do this for me before you go? It's very important.' Or you may exist in a work culture where everyone puts in extra hours. Clock off at 5.30 and you're letting the side down. You're busy because of work expectations. Or maybe it's the expectations of friends. 'Can you do me a favour?' 'See you Friday night.' 'It won't take long.' The test is this: have you ever wanted to say 'No', but said 'Yes'? A teacher told me: 'I feel no great desire to fill my life with activities, but you feel pressure from other people to do things.'

My wife is a fan of Jane Austen. There's nothing she likes better than sitting in a hot bath, reading *Mansfield Park* for the 27th time. I've only managed to read a couple of the Austen novels – with great pleasure I should add. But I get confused about which two novels they are since the plots are so similar. It is, of course, shameful not to have read all the novels of

Jane Austen. And the novels of Thomas Hardy, George Eliot, Anthony Trollope and Charles Dickens. What – you've not read *Ulysses* by James Joyce! And that's just the dead people. How will you hold your own at dinner parties if you've not read the Booker prize shortlist? And you need a working knowledge of popular music; the less popular the popular music the better. It's hard work being a 'culture vulture'. It takes long hours of dedication – plus an aptitude for bluffing. So much of this is driven not by a delight in literature, films and music, but by the desire to impress others. We want to hold our own in the competition to be culturally cool. We don't want to be exposed. We're afraid of what others might think of us.

Churches too can place all sorts of expectations on us. I once talked to a young woman who was tyrannized by the expectations of people at church. No-one told her what she should do, but she picked up their disappointment. Attending prayer meetings, partnering others in evangelism, opening her home for meetings. Now she was in tears. She felt trapped by other people's expectations. Someone else once told me: 'I really don't like saying "No" to people, so I say "I'm busy".' Robert Banks (1983) says:

> If you lack assurance of your acceptability and worth, the temptation is to try to earn approval both from others and yourself by your own efforts. The easiest way to go about this is by doing additional things for them. This is one reason why people take on so many extra tasks and responsibilities that God never required of them. This is why some continue to do more in their churches than they really need to.

We get roughly 80% of our outcomes from roughly 20% of our inputs, according to what is known as Pareto's

Principle or the 80/20 Rule. It seems to hold good in all sorts of areas. So why not apply this rule to your life by settling for that 80% you get from 20% of your time? Take preparing a sermon as an example, although the principles could apply to almost anything. After four hours you have a first draft. Let's say it's 80% as good as it could be. The more work you do on it, the better it will be. But the pay off for your work will quickly diminish. After another four hours you may have got your sermon up to 90%. Why not settle for 80% and spend those four hours doing something else? We should give God 100% of our lives, but that doesn't mean every sermon has to be 100%. We need to view ministry as a whole and think how our time is best used. The point is we are finite and we can't do everything at 100%. I remember someone bemoaning how many church leaders in the United States leave their ministries in their fifties. His explanation was that each week they were trying to hit 100%. Their sermons were being evaluated, judged, rated. Each week required perfection and eventually it took its toll and they bailed out. His conclusion: 40 years of 80% is better than 15 years of 100%. So why don't we settle for 80%? Because we fear other people's disapproval. We want to look good. And so we become perfectionists and perfectionism makes you very busy!

So if we are doing more than we can to meet other people's expectations then we're saying: other people's approval matters more to me than God's.

The lie: other people matter more than God

Remember: *God does not expect me to do more than I can do*. So if we *are* doing more than we can to meet other people's expectations then we're saying: *other people's approval matters more to me than God's*. We crave their approval or fear their rejection. We 'need' the acceptance of others and so we're controlled by them. We 'cannot' say 'No'.

The Bible's term for this is 'fear of man'. *'Fear of man will prove to be a snare, but whoever trusts in the LORD is kept safe'* (Proverbs 29:25). When we can't say 'No' we fear other people more than we fear God. Ed Welch, in his book *When People are Big and God is Small*, says fear of man has many symptoms: susceptibility to peer pressure; 'needing' something from a spouse; a concern with self-esteem; fear of being exposed; small lies to make yourself look good; people making you jealous, angry, depressed or anxious; avoiding people; comparing yourself to others; and fear of evangelism. But one test of fear of man is this: 'Are you over-committed? Do you find it is hard to say no even when wisdom indicates that you should?' (Welch, 1997).

Our culture tries to overcome this problem by finding ways to bolster self-esteem. According to a survey by the Chartered Institute of Personnel and Development, 38% of those working long hours say it brings improved self-esteem. But this actually compounds the problem. We become dependent on whatever or whoever will boost our self-esteem. In reality low self-esteem is thwarted pride – we don't have the status we think we deserve. We elevate often good desires (for love, affirmation, respect) to needs without which we think we cannot be whole. We think we 'need' the approval or acceptance of other people. But our true need is to glorify God and love other people. We should recognize fear of man for what it is, argues Welch: a form of idolatry. 'We exalt other people and their perceived power above God. We worship them as either ones who have God-like exposing gazes (shame-fear) or God-like ability to "fill" us with esteem, love, admiration, acceptance, respect and other psychological desires (reject-ion-fear) . . . They are worshipped because we perceive that they have power to give us something. We think they can bless us' (Welch, 1997). As a result we are enslaved by our fears.

In the next chapter we will discover that if you're busy trying to meet other people's needs then you have made *your-self* their god and saviour. In this chapter we see that if you are busy trying to meet other people's expectations then you have made *other people* your god and saviour. But in both cases the underlying idol is self. When we 'need' approval and affir-mation from other people we are, in effect, wanting them to worship us.

The truth: God alone is my Master

The answer is to repent of our idolatry and turn to God. We need a big view of God. We need to fear God. *'He will be the sure foundation for your times,'* says Isaiah, *'a rich store of salva-tion and wisdom and knowledge; the fear of the LORD is the key to this treasure'* (Isaiah 33:6). The key to God's treasure is to fear him. To fear God is to respect, worship, trust and submit to God. The fear of God is the response to his glory, holiness, power and wrath. The fear of the Lord is recognizing that he is so awesome, powerful, holy and good that we should serve and worship him more than anything or anyone.

The appearances of God are often described in the Bible in terms of brightness, fire and brilliance. Think of the heat of the sun, with nuclear reactions going on within it creating a blinding brilliance even millions of miles away. Yet there is an intensity and substance to God far beyond our sun. When Moses came down from Mount Sinai having met with God, his face was shining so much with just the reflected glory of God that the people were afraid. God wraps majesty and splendour around him like a cloak (Psalm 93:1). '"To whom will you compare me? Or who is my equal?" says the Holy One' (Isaiah 40:25). The fear of God for the Christian no longer involves terror. He is our Father and we come before him with confidence through the mediation of Christ (Hebrews 4:14–16). But we can never get chummy or complacent with him. He remains a consuming fire. 'My flesh trembles in fear of you,' says the Psalmist. 'I stand in awe of your laws' (Psalm 119:120).

So if you are busy because of other people's expectations or you can't say 'no' to people then you need to learn the fear of the LORD. For the fear of God can be taught and learnt (Deuteronomy 4:10; 17:18–19; 31:12; Psalm 34:9–11). Meditate on God's glory, greatness, holiness, power, splendour, beauty, grace, mercy and love. Often, in Psalms 18 and 34 for example, this is what the Psalmist is doing. In the face of some threat he is speaking the truth about God to himself. He is reminding himself of God's greatness so that fear of others is replaced by trust in God. 'I sought the LORD, and he answered me; he delivered me from all my fears. Those who look to him are radiant; their faces are never covered with shame' (Psalm 34:4–5).

And this fear is liberating. It is liberating because it sets us free from every other fear. 'The fear of the LORD leads to life: Then one rests content, untouched by trouble' (Proverbs 19:23; see also 14:26). The fear of God leads to 'rest'. Fearing God sets us free from the frantic busyness that is driven by the desire to please others.

The fear of God is liberating in two ways. First, whenever we're faced with a choice between doing what pleases a person and doing what pleases God, if we truly fear God then we will do what pleases him. 'Do not be afraid of those who kill the body but cannot kill the soul,' says Jesus. 'Rather, be afraid of the One who can destroy both soul and body in hell' (Matthew

10:28). We are no longer controlled by other people's expectations. We are controlled instead by God's expectations. 'Fear him, ye saints, and you will then have nothing else to fear; make you his service your delight your wants shall be his care' (see Tate and Brady). We are servants of God and his service is freedom.

We still serve other people. That's why we've been set free (Galatians 5:13). We take other people's expectations seriously because we want to love them as God commanded. But we're not enslaved by them. We don't serve them for what they can give us in return – approval, affection, security or whatever. We serve them for Christ's sake. By submitting to his lordship, we're free to serve others in love. When people are disappointed in us we need to be able to say to God: 'I'm sorry they're disappointed, but it doesn't matter because I've done what you expect of me.'

Second, the fear of God sets us free because God promises to care for those who fear him.

The angel of the LORD
encamps around those who fear him,
and he delivers them.
Taste and see that the LORD is good;
blessed is the man who takes refuge in him.
Fear the LORD, you his saints,
for those who fear him lack nothing (Psalm 34:7–9).

Life may not always be easy, but God will work for our good in all things and bring us safely home to glory. Fear in the face of threat is natural. Your boss may be fearsome. They may be a bully. But they're not bigger than God. Natural fear needs to be regulated by faith in God. David had good cause to fear others at various points in his life, but he could say:

The LORD is my light and my salvation –
whom shall I fear?
The LORD is the stronghold of my life –
of whom shall I be afraid?
When evil men advance against me
to devour my flesh,
when my enemies and my foes attack me,
they will stumble and fall.
Though an army besiege me,
my heart will not fear;
though war break out against me,
even then will I be confident (Psalm 27:1–3).

When I am afraid,
I will trust in you.
In God, whose word I praise,
in God I trust; I will not be afraid.
What can mortal man do to me? (Psalm 56:3–4)

A victorious heart – a meditation on Psalm 18

The final verse of this Psalm tells us it is about David and his descendants. David was God's anointed king (his 'christ' – the word 'christ' means 'anointed one'). The promise of a King and Saviour over God's people is fulfilled in David's greatest descendant: Jesus Christ. So the person who speaks in this Psalm is Christ. And we are *in Christ*. So in Christ we can make this Psalm our own.

I love you, O LORD, my strength.
² The LORD is my rock, my fortress and my deliverer;
my God is my rock, in whom I take refuge.

He is my shield and the horn of my salvation, my stronghold.
³ I call to the LORD, who is worthy of praise,
and I am saved from my enemies.

List the words David uses to describe the LORD. Each time he says '*my* strength . . . *my* rock . . .' reread the verses replacing 'my' with your name. 'The LORD is Tim's rock . . .'

⁴ The cords of death entangled me;
the torrents of destruction overwhelmed me.
⁵ The cords of the grave coiled around me;
the snares of death confronted me.

You may not be facing death. But think about the times when you feel overwhelmed or when you feel entangled by your commitments. This is a Psalm for those times.

⁶ In my distress I called to the LORD . . .
⁸ Smoke rose from his nostrils;
consuming fire came from his mouth,
burning coals blazed out of it.
⁹ He parted the heavens and came down;
dark clouds were under his feet . . .
¹² Out of the brightness of his presence clouds advanced,
with hailstones and bolts of lightning.
¹³ The LORD thundered from heaven;
the voice of the Most High resounded.
¹⁴ He shot his arrows and scattered the enemies,
great bolts of lightning and routed them.
¹⁵ The valleys of the sea were exposed
and the foundations of the earth laid bare
at your rebuke, O LORD,
at the blast of breath from your nostrils.

God comes in response to David's prayer and what a coming it is! Meditate on all the images that David uses. This is a God to be feared. Think about the times when you can't say 'No'. Think about the people whose acceptance or approval you feel you need. Picture them side by side with God. Who is most to be feared? And look what this thundering, fire-breathing, earth-shattering God does when he arrives . . .

> [16] *He reached down from on high and took hold of me;*
> *he drew me out of deep waters.*
> [17] *He rescued me from my powerful enemy,*
> *from my foes, who were too strong for me.*
> [18] *They confronted me in the day of my disaster,*
> *but the LORD was my support.*
> [19] *He brought me out into a spacious place;*
> *he rescued me because he delighted in me.*

The fearsome God gently takes hold of us, rescues us, supports us, delights in us. Imagine what this might look like in your work or home situation.

> [20] *The LORD has dealt with me according to my righteousness;*
> *according to the cleanness of my hands he has rewarded me . . .*
> [25] *To the faithful you show yourself faithful,*
> *to the blameless you show yourself blameless,*
> [26] *to the pure you show yourself pure,*
> *but to the crooked you show yourself shrewd.*
> [27] *You save the humble*
> *but bring low those whose eyes are haughty.*

As we read these verses we need to remember that they are fulfilled in Jesus. We read them as those who are in Christ and in Christ we can make them our own for in Christ we have been declared righteous. We can say, *'The* LORD *has dealt with me according to* Christ's *righteousness; according to the cleanness of* Christ's *hands he has rewarded me.'* In Christ we are faithful, blameless and pure. And so in Christ God shows himself to us as:

- faithful – he keeps his promises to you
- blameless – when you look back from eternity you won't be able to fault him
- pure – his actions toward you are without any malice

[28] You, O LORD, *keep my lamp burning;*
my God turns my darkness into light.
[29] With your help I can advance against a troop;
with my God I can scale a wall.
[30] As for God, his way is perfect;
the word of the LORD *is flawless.*
He is a shield for all who take refuge in him.
[31] For who is God besides the LORD?
And who is the Rock except our God?
[32] It is God who arms me with strength
and makes my way perfect.
[33] He makes my feet like the feet of a deer;
he enables me to stand on the heights.
[34] He trains my hands for battle;
my arms can bend a bow of bronze.
[35] You give me your shield of victory,
and your right hand sustains me;
you stoop down to make me great.
[36] You broaden the path beneath me,
so that my ankles do not turn over . . .
[39] You armed me with strength for battle;

you made my adversaries bow at my feet . . .
⁴⁶ The LORD lives! Praise be to my Rock!
Exalted be God my Saviour! . . .
⁴⁹ . . . I will praise you among the nations, O LORD;
I will sing praises to your name.
⁵⁰ He gives his king great victories;
he shows unfailing kindness to his anointed,
to David and his descendants for ever.

These words are ultimately about David's descendant Jesus. God has given him a kingdom over the whole earth. And we are in Christ. We may not win every battle, but we are on the victory side. God doesn't guarantee his people an easy life. God doesn't promise that you will clinch the deal, raise a well-behaved child, win promotion, enjoy good health. David spent much of his life as a fugitive and Jesus had to endure the cross. But *'in all these things we are more than conquerors through him who loved us'* (Romans 8:37). God can set you free from the tyranny of other people's expectations. He can set you free to live with him alone as your Master. When you get frantic trying to win someone's approval, remember you are part of a bigger story. Tell your heart you're on the victory side. When you feel overwhelmed or fearful of other people's reactions, turn to this psalm for strength. Use these verses to pray for your situation.

9. I'M BUSY BECAUSE OTHERWISE THINGS GET OUT OF CONTROL – *THE LIBERATING RULE OF GOD*

A friend of mine is involved in missionary work. A few years ago he burnt out, had a breakdown and spent two years on Prozac. 'I thought I could do everything,' he told me. 'I could take on anything and make it happen just by working hard.'

The lie: I can be in control

One of the features of the modern age is its attempt to control nature. Many benefits have come from this. Our fields yield more crops, fewer diseases prove fatal, and so on. Our ability to control nature means, however, that we also have the ability to exploit nature. Modern culture shows the same attitude towards time. Time has become something to manage. The promise is this: you can be in control of your life. Diaries, planners, wall charts, filofaxes – these are the tools by which we assert our sovereignty over time. Now they are being augmented by a new generation of tools: digital organizers, laptop computers, mobile phones, online schedules.

One of the lies that drives our busyness is the belief that we can do everything and solve every problem – it is just a matter of squeezing it all in. The reality is that we are finite. Only God is infinite. Only God is truly in control. We think the solution is a course on time management. But the solution is recognizing that we are human and God is God. We need to trust to him our welfare and the welfare of others.

The truth: the liberating rule of God

Isaiah 28:16 says: *'the one who trusts will never be dismayed'*. The word 'dismayed' is literally 'hurried'. The issue at stake is whether, in the face of the threat from Assyria, the people of God will ally themselves with Egypt or trust in the Lord? Isaiah calls their alliance with Egypt *'a covenant with death'* (verses 15 and 18). It will be swept away and in its place God will establish a kingdom built on the firm foundation of Christ (verses 16–17 and 1 Peter 2:4–8). Those who trust in the foundation of Christ will never be 'hurried'. The image is of people in a flap, rushing to and fro in search of a solution. Perhaps Isaiah has in mind the nation's diplomats scurrying off to Egypt. The people should have heeded God's promise: *'"This is the resting-place, let the weary rest"; and, "This is the place of repose" – but they would not listen'* (verse 12). If they had trusted God they would have found rest and repose. But they wouldn't trust God and so they get in a flap. Doug Sherman and William Hendricks argue that people who get work out of perspective do so because deep down they believe that 'God either cannot or will not provide' and that therefore they themselves must do so through their work. 'No one can rest holding such as belief,' they add. 'No one can enjoy peace and freedom in the presence of such a conviction' (Sherman and Hendricks, 1987).

When Jesus tells us in Luke 12 not to run after the things that make the pagan world so busy, he chides us for our little faith (verse 28). The writer of Proverbs invites us to consider the ant and work hard (Proverbs 6:6–11). But Jesus invites us to *'consider how the lilies grow. They do not labour or spin. Yet I tell you, not even Solomon in all his splendour was dressed like one of these'* (verse 27). Labour is good, but labour which betrays a lack of trust in God's ability to provide for his children is idolatrous. Only through faith in the God who dresses flowers can we seek first the kingdom of God (verse 31). To those who overwork because we are worried things will spin out of control, Jesus poses the question: *'Who of you by worrying can add a single hour to his life?'* (verse 25). We can't add a single hour to our lives, let alone an hour to every day. But there's no need to worry. Our heavenly Father is in control. He requires of us no more than we can do in the time he gives. And the problems we think we need more time to fix are all within his sovereign care. This truth has wonderful power to liberate us from unrealistic expectations.

One thing that drives overwork is job insecurity. There is a strong correlation between insecurity and long hours. Ever since the restructuring of the 1980s, workers have felt less job security. I say 'felt' because perception and reality are divergent. The average length of time spent in a job in Britain for all types of work actually increased significantly during the 1990s. We think our jobs are insecure, but they are more secure. One factor behind this divergence is that job insecurity has affected management and professional positions more than before, making it more interesting to a middle-class-dominated media. Another factor is the routine use of appraisals. Workers' performance is constantly being monitored and assessed. Restructuring is also more common so, even if you don't lose your job, your position may change.

The Sabbath was a reminder that blessing in the land was God's gift. The Sabbath day was part of a wider series of Sabbath regulations in which slaves were freed, debts forgiven and land left fallow. Observing these laws required trust in God as provider. Enforced inactivity made God's people realize that frenetic human work wouldn't provide security. Blessing lay in submission to, and trust in, the rule of God. 'The Sabbath announces that the world is safely in God's hands. The world will not disintegrate if we stop our efforts. The world relies on God's promises and not on our efforts' (Brueggemann, 1982). Constant work is the behaviour of someone who thinks everything depends on them. Rest is the behaviour of someone who looks to God to provide.

Professor Michael Marmot has been tracking the health of civil servants for the past thirty years. He's found that the higher in the hierarchy a person is, the less they suffer from work-related stress. Wider lifestyle issues like smoking and diet only account for a quarter of the difference. 'What turns out to be bad for health,' comments Professor Marmot, 'is not how much demand you have, but how much control you have over the demand and over your working conditions in general' (Marmot, 2004). Another study found that commuters experience greater levels of stress than fighter pilots and riot police. 'The difference is that a riot policeman or a combat pilot have things they can do to combat the stress . . . But commuters, particularly on a train, cannot do anything about it at all.' I can't move you up the hierarchy or get your train moving. But I can tell you the good news that your heavenly Father is in control of your life. Next time you are stuck in traffic, don't fret about the missed appointment. Meditate on the sovereign goodness of your heavenly Father. Give thanks that his plan for you is best, even if it's not your plan. We want to be in control. We need to let God be in control. We want to rule our lives. We need to let God rule our lives.

What, asks Tom Wright, is the most common command in the Bible? Be good? Be holy? Don't sin? 'No. The most frequent command in the Bible is: *"Don't be afraid." Don't be afraid. Fear not, don't be afraid.* The irony of this surprising command is that, though it's what we all really want to hear, we have as much difficulty, if not more, in obeying this command as any other' (Wright, 1994). Believing in the God who raised Christ from the dead means 'believing that it is going to be all right; and this belief is, ultimately, incompatible with fear . . . Though we may at any stage in our lives grasp the truth that God raised Jesus from the dead, it takes us all our life long to let that belief soak through and permeate the rest of our thinking, feeling, and worrying lives.' In other words, the test of faith is not assent to the bodily resurrection of Jesus (important as that is). It is whether trust in the God of resurrection slows down our frenetic worry-induced busyness. *'You will keep in perfect peace him whose mind is steadfast, because he trusts in you'* (Isaiah 26:3). John White (1979) says: 'We must be suspicious of any faith about personal justification that is not substantiated by faith in God's power over material things in our everyday life. Faith about pie in the sky when I die cannot be demonstrated. Faith that God can supply my need today can be demonstrated.'

Come Sleep!
Despite a prodigious output, the English writer Samuel Johnson wished he could get up earlier. He writes in his journal of his resolve to 'to rise early, not later than six if I can'. It was a resolution that clearly eluded him for a year later he writes: 'I purpose to rise at eight because though I shall not yet rise early it will be much earlier than I now rise,

for I often lye till two.' Perhaps his experience is something you can relate to. How many times have you decided to get up regularly an hour earlier? How many times have you succeeded?

There is an assumption in Christian circles that it's more godly to get up early to pray than it is to sleep. After all, reducing your sleep to seven hours a night would gain you an additional three years of time over a lifetime. We are regaled with stories of saints from past centuries who rose at five to pray (forgetting that most went to bed soon after dark). This is what happens when I get up early to pray over a period of time: I get tired. (It's not rocket science!) And when I get tired, I get grumpy, irritable and selfish. I sin. Tiredness is not an excuse for these sins, but like a recovering alcoholic avoiding the pub, it makes sense for me to avoid getting tired. Of course, sometimes it's appropriate to pray through the night just as Jesus did (Luke 6:12). And people are different. I need eight hours sleep a night, while other people get away with less. But here's the deal: God made human beings and he built in a need to sleep. People who think they can operate with little sleep are defying God's created order. God's first priority for a despondent Elijah was plenty of sleep and hearty meals (1 Kings 19:5–9). Next time someone makes you feel inadequate with their talk of early rising, think of Colossians 2:23: '*Such regulations indeed have an appearance of wisdom, with their self-imposed worship, their false humility and their harsh treatment of the body, but they lack any value in restraining sensual indulgence.*' If you want to find time to pray why not switch off the television? But don't try to give up sleep – not over a period of time. God didn't make you to miss sleep. Sleeping is not unrighteous. God gave us sleep as a gift. One of the favourite poems in our home is Philip Sidney's sonnet to sleep, which begins:

Come, Sleep; O Sleep! the certain knot of peace,
The baiting-place of wit, the balm of woe,
The poor man's wealth, the prisoner's release,
Th' indifferent judge between the high and low.

Trusting God for others

'I'm busy because people need me.' It's another version of 'I'm busy because otherwise things get out of control.' If I'm not active then things will get out of control in someone else's life. We Christians have our own well-motivated version of this. We assume any need implies a responsibility on us to meet it. 'Something ought to be done,' we say. The pressure comes from hyper-active people in a constant fever of disappointment that more isn't happening. But we are human. We are not God. We shouldn't over-estimate ourselves – we are *not* indispensable. We like to think we can solve every problem, but we cannot. Even if we have the ability to help, we can't help everyone.

> *We are not God. We shouldn't over-estimate ourselves – we are not indispensable. We like to think we can solve every problem, but we cannot.*

Pauline gives herself in the service of others. If people need someone to talk to, or need help with their shopping, as often as not she's the one to whom they turn. She's always cheerful, patient, willing. She's also often tired. We talk about her struggle to cope. She wishes other people were in a position to share the load. Some people need to be urged to do more for God. But I keep telling her to do less. She needs to learn to say 'No'. 'But what can I do?' she asks. 'They need help.'

But you are not the Messiah. You are not anyone's Saviour. We have a responsibility to serve others, but we don't have a responsibility to save them – that's God's job. A charity executive emailed: 'If we're getting over-tired and stressed and not giving our best to our families (I'm guilty of this I'm told) then we should prayerfully consider how to pull back and let God fill the gap, because he is sovereign and he provides. He will provide others to fill the gap we have left.' The question is: do we believe God is sovereign and that he provides? We can assent easily to the truth, but does it shape the way we live?

Don't get me wrong. We have a responsibility to serve God and love other people. Paul spoke of *'being poured out like a drink offering on the sacrifice and service coming from your faith'* (Philippians 2:17). He commended his hard work as a model for others (2 Thessalonians 3:8–9). We are to be poured out in service. We are to give until there is nothing left to give. But then we stop. We cannot and should not do more than we can. God doesn't expect it of us. We are not saviours. He alone is the Saviour.

Colin is a youth leader in his local church – a role he combines with a secular job. On both counts he was overworking so that he had no time to spend with his fiancée. Eventually he was told by his pastor to stop his involvement in youth work and sort out his relationship with his wife-to-be. But he couldn't! So he ended up lying to his pastor about how much he was actually doing. On one occasion he visited his fiancée's family for the weekend. He spent the days with them, but then worked through the night on his laptop. The following weekend he went to a Christian conference. He works as if the future of the young people depends on him. Now his fiancée is questioning whether or not they should get married.

Listen to Paul's words in 2 Corinthians 4. They're words of sanity and rest for us in our Christian service.

> *Therefore, since through God's mercy we have this ministry, we do not lose heart.* *²Rather, we have renounced secret and shameful ways; we do not use deception, nor do we distort the word of God. On the contrary, by setting forth the truth plainly we commend ourselves to every man's conscience in the sight of God.* *³And even if our gospel is veiled, it is veiled to those who are perishing.* *⁴The god of this age has blinded the minds of unbelievers, so that they cannot see the light of the gospel of the glory of Christ, who is the image of God.* *⁵For we do not preach ourselves, but Jesus Christ as Lord, and ourselves as your servants for Jesus' sake.* *⁶For God, who said, 'Let light shine out of darkness,' made his light shine in our hearts to give us the light of the knowledge of the glory of God in the face of Christ* (2 Corinthians 4:1–6).

Why do people reject the gospel message? Would people respond

- if I spent more hours on my talks, polishing the prose, finding telling illustrations, making it punchier?
- if I spent more time with the young people in my church, planning fun activities, hanging out with them, running Bible studies, organizing Christian concerts?
- if I deceived people or distorted God's word (verse 2) or projected myself as a dynamic, compelling leader (verse 5)?

No, says Paul. The reason people don't respond is that they've been blinded (verses 3–4). People will only respond to the gospel if God opens their eyes. God must do a work of recreation just as he first created light through his word (verse 6). That doesn't mean we're left with nothing to do.

Our job is to set forth the truth plainly and preach Jesus Christ as Lord (verses 2 and 5). We are to speak the word by which God opens blind eyes (verse 6). Our job is proclamation; conversion is God's job. And we should work hard at our job. We should pour ourselves into it. But we must never confuse our job with God's job. That's madness. If we ever think conversion depends on us, then we will step out onto the road to burnout. We need to trust God, praying for the salvation of others while accepting that both salvation and judgment are his prerogative. This is the truth that enables us not to lose heart (verse 1).

Trust and obey

Paul Tripp (2002) talks about the circle of responsibility and the circle of concern. The circle of responsibility contains those things that are important to me and which I can influence. I have a responsibility to be a godly spouse, parent, child and friend. I have a responsibility to proclaim Christ and serve in his church. My duty with respect to things in the circle of responsibility is to obey God. Around this is a wider circle – the circle of concern. This contains the things that are important to me, but which are beyond my ability to change. This includes things like love from a spouse, the conversion of a friend, financial security for my family and so on. My duty with respect to the circle of concern is to trust God.

Problems arise when people confuse the two circles. Some people put things that should be in the circle of responsibility into the circle of concern. In other words, they expect God to do their job for them because they are lazy or shirk responsibility. Other people put things that should be in the circle of concern into the circle of responsibility. They take responsibility for things for which they should trust God. This leads to busyness and worry. Worry is accepting responsibility that

God never intended you to have. I have a responsibility to be a serving, sacrificial and loving husband. But I don't have a responsibility to make my wife love me. People can wear themselves out trying to earn other people's love. I have a responsibility to proclaim Christ to people, but I must trust God for their conversion. I have a responsibility to commend the gospel at work, but I must trust God for my boss's attitude to me. If I take responsibility for my boss's attitude then my work may overwhelm me. We create stress for ourselves when we move things from our circle of concern into our circle of responsibility. Jesus says: *'Do not worry about tomorrow, for tomorrow will worry about itself'* (Matthew 6:34). Everything in tomorrow is by definition in the circle of concern not the circle of responsibility, since we cannot influence it yet. I should obey today instead of worrying about tomorrow.

Readers of a certain age will remember the song: 'Trust and obey, for there's no other way to be happy in Jesus, but to trust and obey.' We trust God for our concerns and obey God in our responsibilities. Don't take responsibility for those things you should leave to God. You'll end up playing god. And God is a much better God than you are! You will soon burn yourself out. *'He will not let your foot slip – he who watches over you will not slumber; indeed, he who watches over Israel will neither slumber nor sleep'* (Psalm 121:3–4).

'There's no other way to be happy in Jesus, but to trust and obey.' It's not that all the things in your circle of concern will turn out the way you want them to. That's not the happiness that's promised. But if you want to be 'happy in Jesus', then trust his love, power and wisdom. Things may not turn out the way you want, but they will turn out for your good. A widow raised a large family including twelve adopted children and through it all managed to maintain stability. A newspaper reporter asked how she had managed. She replied:

'Because I'm in a partnership. Many years ago I said, "Lord, I'll do the work and you do the worrying."'

'I'm busy because otherwise things get out of control' is a lie. The truth is that God is my heavenly Father.

※

A restful heart – a meditation on Psalm 127

Unless the LORD builds the house,
its builders labour in vain.
Unless the LORD watches over the city,
the watchmen stand guard in vain.

We like to think that if we just work hard enough then we can be sure of building the company, growing the church, raising the family, achieving our goals. And if things go pear-shaped then a bit more effort and we can solve the problem. But unless the LORD builds or watches, it's all in vain. We are running after what cannot be attained. No wonder we're worn out! We're busy, busy, busy because we think it depends on us. There's no rest for the wicked heart that trusts its own efforts instead of trusting God. What are you 'building'? Do you think success is simply a question of effort? Do you think problems can be solved by working harder?

[2] *In vain you rise early*
and stay up late,
toiling for food to eat –
for he grants sleep to those he loves.

In the New Living Translation this verse reads: *'It is useless for you to work so hard from early morning to late at night, anxiously working for food to eat.'* What is the Bible's verdict on getting up early? It's useless! Getting up early is a waste of time if you think you can use the extra time to achieve your goals, solve your problems, control your life. Far from being virtuous, to work when we should sleep betrays a lack of trust in God. Psalms 3 and 4 were written when David was deposed by his own son. Yet in both he speaks of sleeping in peace because God sustains him and makes him dwell in safety (3:5 and 4:8). Robert Banks (1983) says: 'Transgressing the limits of environmental rhythms can be an act of unbelief, a reliance upon human works rather than on God's provision.' Think about the last time you worked beyond your normal bedtime or set the alarm an hour earlier. What drove you to do it? What was the attitude of your heart towards God in that moment?

When was the last time you lay awake at night worrying? God has a gift for you if you will only trust him – the gift of sleep. He gives rest to our restless hearts. A possible translation of verse 2 is: *'For while they sleep God provides for those he loves'* (NIV footnote). It's a lovely image: while we sleep secure in God's sovereign care, he is at work on our behalf providing for our needs.

³ Sons are a heritage from the LORD,
children a reward from him.
⁴ Like arrows in the hands of a warrior
are sons born in one's youth.
⁵ Blessed is the man
whose quiver is full of them.
They will not be put to shame
when they contend with their enemies in the gate.

These verses appear unrelated to verses 1–2 until you realize that in the culture of the time children represented security for the future. They would provide for you in old age and offer legal protection (verse 5). What is the source of your security for the future? Are you over-working to obtain a secure future?

There may be another link between the two halves of this Psalm. In 2 Samuel 7 David proposes to build a house (a temple) for the LORD. The LORD responds by promising to build a house (a dynasty) for David. This is a Psalm 'of Solomon', David's son and the builder of the temple. As Solomon listens to the builders working on the temple in the city of David, he reflects that God's kingdom doesn't depend on their success. It rests on God's promise that David's family will always reign over God's people. And your future rests on Jesus the Son of David. And Jesus said: *'I am the vine; you are the branches. If a man remains in me and I in him, he will bear much fruit; apart from me you can do nothing'* (John 15:5).

10. I'M BUSY BECAUSE I PREFER BEING UNDER PRESSURE – *THE LIBERATING REFUGE OF GOD*

Have you ever worked into the night to meet a deadline? Or got up in the small hours of the morning? Or cancelled appointments in order to work? Or blew out meeting up with friends? 'I'm busy,' you say, 'because I've simply got to get this done and I've only got a couple of days left. I work better under pressure. I'm not busy all the time – just when a deadline looms.'

Sometimes there's a crisis and we just need to get on with it. But most of the time we end up pushing to meet a deadline because we've put off starting. We procrastinate. We don't feel like getting on with unpleasant tasks. Or we feel overwhelmed by large tasks. And so we find other things to do. We check our emails. Tidy our desks. Do our filing. Surf the internet. Make another cup of tea. We work around the task without ever getting on with it. We're not doing the task God has called us to do. As a result we're to blame when we find ourselves in a frantic rush to meet a deadline. We put it off and now it's caught up with us. Sometimes our procrastination is obvious like when we play solitaire on the computer. And sometimes we spend our time doing good things. We answer letters. Visit friends. It looks like we're being diligent. We note all the important things we're getting done. But if we would only be honest with ourselves, they're all ways of putting off the task before us. Procrastination commonly has three stages. See if you recognize them in yourself (adapted from Henegar, 2001):

1. It's not due yet – I've got plenty of time.
2. It's crunch time – I have a right to neglect all my other responsibilities.
3. I've finished the job – I have a right to reward myself.

	URGENT	NOT URGENT
IMPORTANT	*1. Important and urgent* • dealing with crises • pressing problems • deadline-driven projects	*2. Important and not urgent* • crisis prevention • relationship building • recognizing new opportunities • planning and advance preparation • recreation and relaxation • training and learning
UNIMPORTANT	*3. Unimportant and urgent* • most interruptions • some mail, email, phone calls and meetings • requests to which you should have said 'No'	*4. Unimportant and not urgent* • trivia • some mail, email, phone calls and meetings • work avoidance and time-wasting activities

Stephen Covey (1992) draws what he calls 'the time management matrix' (see page 127). He invites us to evaluate tasks according to whether they're important or not and whether they're urgent or not. This allows us to place all our actions in one of four quadrants:

1. Important and urgent
2. Important and not urgent
3. Unimportant and urgent
4. Unimportant and not urgent

List the sorts of activities you do in each quadrant.

We should be focusing our time on Quadrant 2 activities – the ones that are important, but not urgent. Spending time in Quadrants 3 and 4 leads to ineffectiveness. People often spend time in Quadrant 3 thinking they're in Quadrant 1 because we confuse urgency with importance. Studies repeatedly show most managers don't deal with things according to importance, but according to urgency. Of course, we can't neglect Quadrant 1 (reacting to deadlines and managing crises). But spending all our time in Quadrant 1 will lead to stress and burnout. Quadrant 1 will become a never-ending task.

We can shrink the list of urgent tasks that face us (Quadrant 1) by spending more time on the non-urgent, important tasks of Quadrant 2. We need to safeguard time on important matters so that it's the unimportant things that get edged out rather the important ones. Of course, we need to recognize our interdependence with others. Just because something is important doesn't mean that *you* should do it. In the economy of God there may be others who can do it better. Spend your time contributing to God's kingdom the things God has equipped you to do. At the same time, be servant-hearted. Just because something is unimportant to you doesn't mean that it doesn't matter to other people.

We get time for Quadrant 2 activities, argues Covey, by avoiding unimportant activities – activities in Quadrants 3 and 4. The problem is that Quadrant 3 activities and especially Quadrant 4 activities offer an escape from the pressures of the other quadrants. 'Some people are beaten up by problems all day every day,' says Covey. 'The only relief they have is in escaping to the not important, not urgent activities of Quadrant 4 . . . That's how people who manage their lives by crisis live.' We procrastinate because we opt for Quadrant 3 and 4 activities over Quadrant 1 and 2 activities.

The lie: I work better under pressure

The most common excuse for procrastination is: 'I work better under pressure. I need a deadline to focus the mind. I do my best work when the heat's on.' We can even pride ourselves on our ability to pull it off at the last minute. We can knock out the essay with an all-nighter. We can improvise the business presentation. We can work under pressure where others would buckle. But this ignores the fact that most of us have no problem getting on with tasks we enjoy. The 'I-work-better-under-pressure' line somehow doesn't seem to apply to the things we like doing.

More importantly, it ignores the harmful impacts of our procrastination. Children go without parents, wives without husbands. Corners are cut. Co-workers are stressed. Others pick up our responsibilities. Our bodies are strained. And tired minds make us more susceptible to anger, resentment, jealousy and frustration.

When the pressure's on we think: 'I have a right to neglect my other responsibilities because I need to get this done'.

That may be okay when an unexpected crisis has made our busyness unavoidable. But when it's the result of our procrastination it's a dereliction of duty. If you leave everything to the last moment you will let people down. Either you won't deliver or you'll deliver at the expense of others. It's one thing to break a promise to my wife of an evening together because a crisis has occurred. It's quite another thing to do so because I've left some task to the last minute.

The question deadline junkies need to ask is: does leaving things to the last moment produce good fruit or bad fruit? (see Luke 6:43–45). Maybe the pressures focus your mind and you produce good work. But maybe along the way other responsibilities are neglected.

There are two common underlying causes of procrastination: my pleasure and my pride.

First, we can procrastinate because we prioritize our pleasure. Faced by something we don't want to do, we don't do it. Most of the time we procrastinate over tasks we can do – they just require some hard work. Given the choice between pleasure and responsibilities, we choose pleasure. It's a short-term outlook. Our responsibilities catch up with us. But in the moment we choose self.

Second, we can procrastinate because our pride is threatened. Faced by a difficult task, a tough decision, a daunting project, we escape by doing something else. We find smaller, easier tasks. We bolster our flagging pride by giving ourselves jobs we can do easily and successfully. The large task we face makes us feel small and feeble. So we do something, anything, that will make us feel good about ourselves. Procrastination can be a form of escapism. For me it takes a still more sinister form. I retreat into a fantasy world in which I'm an achiever, a top performer, a success. Other people escape by eating. They comfort themselves with chocolate, biscuits or ice cream. Procrastination is pride under threat. It's a proud heart running into difficulty. And so it takes the easy way out. It thrashes about for the first thing that will give it a boost. That may be clearing our email inbox. It may be completing solitaire. It may be creating a fantasy world in which I am god. Procrastinators are not strong people who can cope with pressure. They are weak people whose fragile egos need constant bolstering.

The truth: God is my refuge
So what should we do when we waver between the biscuit tin and the ironing? What should we do as our mouse hovers between solitaire and Word?

First, repent. Acknowledge procrastination for what it is: self-deception, selfishness, escapism, pride. Recognize it as the symptom of a sinful heart. Turn from self back to God. Accept your responsibilities as responsibilities that he has given to you. To reject them is to reject God's authority over you. To postpone them is to put his authority on hold.

Acknowledge procrastination for what it is: self-deception, selfishness, escapism, pride.

Second, place your faith in God as your refuge. We try to escape when we cannot face something. And the reason we cannot face something is that we don't trust God. We take refuge in all the things that make up our procrastination when we should take refuge in God. If you take refuge in God when you feel like running away from daunting tasks then you will avoid the busyness of deadlines. You will discover the rest of those who dwell in the shelter of the Most High:

He who dwells in the shelter of the Most High
will rest in the shadow of the Almighty.
I will say of the LORD, 'He is my refuge and my fortress,
my God, in whom I trust' (Psalm 91:1–2).

The lie: busyness is a refuge

Why do some men who never enter a kitchen, except to ask when dinner will be ready, always take charge of BBQs? It could be the pyromaniac tendencies of their inner child. But I suspect it's often because they prefer busying themselves with the BBQ than making polite conversation with guests. Busyness itself can be a refuge. We can be busy in one area of our lives as a way of hiding from problems in another area. Some people stay late at work, take on business trips or volunteer for extra projects because they prefer work to home. We fill our lives with commitments and activities to avoid facing issues. When we procrastinate we seek refuge *from* busyness and end up more busy. But we can also find refuge *in* busyness itself.

Amanda is a mother with three small children. She works part-time as an office manager in a doctor's surgery. She takes pride in a well-managed office. Her desk is tidy, the day is structured, meetings have agendas. Home on the other hand is chaos. Toys are strewn across the floor, there's jam on the curtains and there are crumbs on the floor. Conversations are constantly interrupted. At work she is smart and clean. At home her clothes are soon covered in sticky finger marks. At work she handles paperwork and deals with adults who are reasonable (most of the time). At home she changes stinking nappies and deals with toddler tantrums. When she gets home, her husband, Bob, immediately hands her the baby. He's frazzled after a day of nappies, baby-talk and noise, and wants a few quiet minutes to prepare the dinner. The practice partners have asked Amanda if she could go full-time. Not surprisingly, it's an attractive prospect.

Colin is the foreman in a garage. He's good at his job and loves the challenge of repairing cars. Each day brings the satisfaction of a job well done. At home he faces the aggro of two rebellious teenagers. The job of bringing up children never seems to be done and he's not sure he's very good at it. At work he's respected. He enjoys a laugh with the lads, but when he shouts they jump. At home when he shouts, his children shout back. And so at five o'clock the prospect of an hour's overtime is seriously appealing.

Peter and Karen have been married for nearly thirty years. To all intents and purposes it's been a successful marriage. Certainly anyone looking in would mark them down as okay. But six months ago their last child left home for university. Both would say that those six months have been a struggle. But not to each other – they don't really talk about their feelings. Raising children kept them preoccupied. They had a common interest, something to talk about. Now they're not sure what their marriage is for. Karen's decided to train as a bereavement counsellor. Peter's taken on extra projects at work. Neither is sure what their motives are, but it's better to be busy than to discover you have nothing to say to your spouse.

The advantage of these ways of avoiding issues is that few people will criticize you for being a conscientious worker. We can even fool ourselves. We pride ourselves in being a good husband and father because we are good breadwinners. But all the time our busyness prevents us from being the husband and father we should be.

The word of God finds no hearing in our restless world. In our hurried lives we have no time to reflect, to think, to meditate on God's word. 'There is not enough silence' for God's word to 'resound'. Dick Clark, presenter of the long-running television show *American Bandstand*, once said 'music is the soundtrack of our lives'. The reality is that television and radio have become the background noise of our lives. We shut out silence to shield ourselves from the big questions. In our living rooms we turn on the television. In our kitchens and our cars we tune in to the radio. Even as we walk along the street we switch on our iPods or talk on mobile phones to the people we're about to visit. We fill our lives with noise and trivia so we can escape the questions and disquiet.

'I'm busy because I prefer being under pressure. Procrastination or busyness is a refuge.' The liberating truth is that God alone is my refuge.

❖

An unshaken heart – a meditation on Psalm 62

My soul finds rest in God alone;
my salvation comes from him.
[2] He alone is my rock and my salvation;
he is my fortress, I shall never be shaken.
[3] How long will you assault a man?
Would all of you throw him down –
this leaning wall, this tottering fence?
[4] They fully intend to topple him
from his lofty place;
they take delight in lies.
With their mouths they bless,
but in their hearts they curse.

It seems David feared being deposed. People were plotting to bring him down. What do you fear? Is procrastination a refuge from your fears? Do you find some tasks overwhelming?

What activities do you typically do when you're procrastinating? Next time you find yourself doing them, try to identify what you're avoiding. You may find it very revealing! Or is busyness itself a refuge? What problems are you evading?

> *⁵ Find rest, O my soul, in God alone;*
> *my hope comes from him.*
> *⁶ He alone is my rock and my salvation;*
> *he is my fortress, I shall not be shaken.*
> *⁷ My salvation and my honour depend on God;*
> *he is my mighty rock, my refuge.*
> *⁸ Trust in him at all times, O people;*
> *pour out your hearts to him,*
> *for God is our refuge.*

Where do you find refuge when you're overwhelmed? In work avoidance? In escapist fantasies? In busyness itself? None of these gives us rest. In God *alone* our souls find true rest. Look at each time David says 'my'. What does God provide for us? Write these words out and have them to hand next time you look for refuge in other things. Put them by your computer screen or biscuit tin. And pour out your heart to God now in prayer: we find rest when we take refuge in him.

> *¹¹ . . . One thing God has spoken,*
> *two things have I heard:*
> *that you, O God, are strong,*
> *¹² and that you, O Lord, are loving.*

David has learnt two important things about God: he is strong and he is loving. When we face overwhelming tasks or problems we would rather avoid we can be sure of two things: God is able to do us good because he is strong; God plans to do us good because he is loving. Tell your heart these truths when you're tempted to run away from things.

Surely you will reward each person
according to what he has done.

This chapter has been about being busy because we put things off. We can put off difficult tasks until the deadline looms. We can put off dealing with issues by busying ourselves with other activities. If you've been putting something off, now's the time to get on with it!

11. I'M BUSY BECAUSE I NEED THE MONEY
– *THE LIBERATING JOY OF GOD*

Time is money

We use similar words for both time and money: spending, saving, gaining, wanting, wasting, squandering. 'Time is money,' advised Benjamin Franklin in *Advice to a Young Tradesman* (1745). Franklin helped write the Declaration of Independence and US Constitution. And his 'time-is-for-making-money' philosophy has become ingrained in the Western way of life. 'Lunch is for wimps,' said Gordon Gekko in the movie *Wall Street*. Lunch diverts time from the pursuit of money. Time is no longer a gift from God, but a commodity with a price tag.

Yet in our society the adage 'time is money' is to a certain extent true – perhaps because we live in a culture shaped by the vision it encapsulates. There often is a trade-off between time and money. We spend time to gain money. At work we give our time to our employer in return for wages. Time is price tagged at £6 an hour. We also spend time to save money. We engage in DIY instead of paying a builder or decorator. And we can also spend money to gain time. We buy ready-cooked meals, non-iron clothes, disposable nappies. We pay cleaners, builders, car washers to do work for us.

We can make choices that give us more time. We can choose to spend less time working and content ourselves with less income. Not all overtime has to be worked. Not all contracts have to be accepted. Not every promotion has to be taken. If all else fails, you can always switch jobs. We can choose to spend less time shopping. Professor Barry Schwartz (2004) distinguishes between what he calls 'maximizers' and 'satisfiers'. Maximizers are concerned to get the best deal. They spend hours looking for the best product for the cheapest price. But the process does not satisfy. It leads to regret when a better deal comes out. 'Satisfiers' in contrast settle for 'good enough'. They find what they want and buy it straight away. They suffer less regret and waste less time.

Are we busy because we need the money? The evidence doesn't bear this out for long hours are not primarily a problem for the low paid. It might have been true in the 1890s when the poorest worked harder than the rich. But by 1991 the richest 10% of Americans spent more hours working than the poorest (Bunting, 2004). Some people have to work long hours to make ends meet. But the demographic of Christian readers suggests that few people reading this book are in that position.

The lie: material possessions can satisfy

The problem is we don't think we can live on less. In 1989 *Time* magazine ran a cover story entitled: 'How America Has Run Out of Time'. The article blamed our economic expectations. A quarter of those working long hours say they do so to maintain their standard of living (Chartered Institute of Personnel and Development, 2000). Journalist Carl Honoré (2004) says: 'Why are so many of us working so hard? One reason is money. Everyone needs to earn a living, but the endless hunger for consumer goods means that we need more and more cash.' The priority of money over time is reflected in the reasons why people look for new jobs. While 8% of those looking for another job want to work fewer hours, 25% are after more pay (*Social Trends*, 2005).

We really do think we need our present incomes. That's because we assume we need the affluent lifestyle to which everyone else aspires. Madeleine Bunting (2004) comments:

> If someone complains about having to work too hard, sooner or later they'll say that they have 'no choice'. Probe a little further, and what becomes clear is that for much of the workforce living well above the poverty line, the connection between pay and overwork is about aspiration to particular patterns of consumption. This is murky territory where one person's 'needs' are 'desires' to another. Are mobile phones, foreign holidays and DVD players luxuries or necessities of contemporary living? The perceived lack of choice may be the consequence of a series of choices – the bigger house, the new car, the rising debt – which trap people into carrying on working very hard.

Notice the language that she uses. We are trapped by our choices. We are enslaved by the lie of consumerism. Tom Hodgkinson (2004) says: 'The advertising industry leads us to believe that life will be improved by the purchase of a product. The purchase of a product requires money. Money requires hard work. Or debt. We go into debt to chase our desires, and then keep working to pay the debt. It's the modern form of indentured labour.'

Our culture says that wealth, possessions and shopping are the route to satisfaction and fulfilment. But it's a lie. Studies show that people in acute poverty are less happy than the better off. But once basic needs are met, more wealth does not equate to more happiness. In the past 30 years, the national income of the United States has more than doubled, but 14 million *fewer* people describe themselves as 'very happy'.

In 1883 James Buchanan Duke bought two Bonsack cigarette making machines. Between them they could produce 240,000 cigarettes a day. The problem was that this was more than the entire population of the United States smoked each day. Between 1859 and 1899 the number of factories in the United States grew from 140,000 to 512,000. Together they were producing more goods than the existing population wanted. Instead of cutting back on production, the new capitalists sought to raise demand. Money-back guarantees, credit, brand names and advertising were introduced to bridge the gap between production and consumption; to turn a culture that valued thrift and home production into a culture that valued spending and consumption. A society that had frowned on greed was now encouraged to pursue ever-increasing economic growth at a national level and ever-rising standards of living at a personal level. Until the nineteenth century advertising had simply conveyed information – much like the classified adverts of today. From the late nineteenth century, adverts were used to create a consumer ethos in which the good life was attained through buying products. People were encouraged to desire – even to 'need' – things they had previously managed happily without. When Henry Crowell of Quaker Oats built an automated mill in 1882, most Americans had meat and potatoes for breakfast. Crowell said his aim in advertising was 'to awaken an interest in and create a demand for cereals where none existed'. Soon adverts weren't simply extolling the attributes of the product itself. Instead they created a range of associations that promised meaning: identity, love and even spirituality. Advertising copywriter

John Starr Hewitt wrote in 1925: 'No one has ever in his life bought a mere piece of merchandise per se. What he buys is the satisfaction of a physical need or the gratification of some dream about his life.'

Advertising tells us that possessions bring satisfaction, fulfilment and identity. But Jesus says: *A man's life does not consist in the abundance of his possessions'* (Luke 12:15). In fact the job of advertising is to make us dissatisfied so that we buy more products. Meanwhile the Bible commends contentment (1 Timothy 6:6–10). We are encouraged to enjoy the good things God has given us without wanting more (1 Timothy 6:17).

We too easily swap the word 'need' for the words 'want', 'desire' or 'lust'. We lust after more money, but tell ourselves we 'need' a pay rise. The truth is we 'need' the pay rise not to live, but to feel good about ourselves. 'Consumerism has become the arena where we develop our sense of self, and experience a sense of freedom,' says Madeleine Bunting (2004). 'It has become the very definition of the good life – we know who we are through our patterns of consumption: our choice of brands, our leisure habits, and so on.' Moreover 'the harder you work, the longer and the more intense your hours, the more pressure you experience, the more intense is the drive to *repair, console, restore,* and *find periodic escape* through consumerism.' We cope with our busy lives by 'giving' ourselves a shopping trip, a manicure, a night out on the town, a restaurant meal.

Our culture is characterized by the question: 'How can I get more?' Christian culture should be asking the opposite question: 'How can I give up more?' Think about the possessions you own and the activities you are involved in. Which could you give up to release time, space and money for God's kingdom? How could you de-clutter your life and home? It was said of Hudson Taylor, 'he enjoyed quietness and the luxury of having few things to take care of'. We need to think

Our culture is characterized by the question: 'How can I get more?' Christian culture should be asking the opposite question: 'How can I give up more?'

of luxury as the carefreeness of having little rather than the burden of having much. We need to reverse the direction of our questions about time and money. Suppose a young person in relation to sex asks, 'How far can I go?' Or a man tempted to an adulterous affair with a particular woman asks, 'How much time can I spend with her?' We would surely urge them to flee from temptation. We would reverse the direction of questioning so that it becomes, 'What can I do to ensure I keep as far from sin as possible?' So it is with consumerism. Christians often ask: 'What is it okay to have?' Why not ask: 'What's the least I can manage with?'

We are all consumers. We need food, clothes, recreation and so on. But in our society we no longer consume to live. Now we live to consume. But we are never satisfied. We cannot be. The adverts can never deliver on their promises. However rapacious our consumption, the next advert we see creates still more dissatisfaction in our hearts. Americans see 3,500 adverts each day. Several times a year the Christian writer Philip Yancey 'disengages' from Western culture, either by visiting a foreign country or by hiking in wilderness. On return, he says, he experiences 'a jolt of re-entry'. 'I watch the commercials promising sexual conquests if I drink a certain beer and professional esteem if I rent from a certain car company. The first day back, modern culture betrays itself as a self-evident lie, a grotesque parody of the day-to-day life I know. The next day my reactions moderate. A few days later I am breathing the air of lust, consumerism, selfishness, and ambition, and it seems normal' (Yancey, 2003). The real challenge for the church is to create a counter-cultural community in which we are *constantly* disengaging from the lies of our materialistic culture.

The truth: the liberating joy of God

It's not enough to 'give up' material possessions. Changing behaviour on its own never lasts (Colossians 2:20–23). We need to change our hearts. We need to rediscover the joy of knowing God. C. S. Lewis (2000) suggests our problem is not that we have desires we want to satisfy, but that we are *too easily* satisfied.

> If we consider the unblushing promises of reward and the staggering nature of the rewards promised in the Gospels, it would seem that our Lord finds our desires, not too strong, but too weak. We are half-hearted creatures, fooling around with drink and sex and ambition when infinite joy is offered us, like an ignorant child who wants to go on making mud pies in a slum because he cannot imagine what is meant by the offer of a holiday at the sea. We are far too easily pleased.

The invitation of the Bible is not to dreary abstinence. It's a call to find in God that which truly satisfies. Living aright in a consumer society is about faith. It's about believing that we find fulfilment, satisfaction, joy and identity in knowing God, and nowhere else.

As Jesus warns us about treasure on earth he also promises us treasure in heaven. Here is the antidote to materialism. Materialism as a philosophy is the belief that this material world is all there is, with no spiritual world, no God, no life after death. Materialism as a way of life is the attempt to find fulfilment from the things of this material world. In an experiment one group of people were asked about their feelings on the prospect of their death while a control group were asked to talk about music (Kasser, 2003). Each group was then asked what they expected to spend on luxury items over the next 15 years. Those who had reflected on their mortality said they anticipated spending an average of $813 per month on entertainment, leisure and clothing. Those who had just been thinking about music anticipated spending $410 a month. Conspicuous consumption would seem in part to be a response to the fear of death. When we think this life is all there is, then we invest in this life. If we're looking forward to the life to come, we'll invest in the treasure of heaven. *'Set your hearts on things above,'* says Paul, *'where Christ is seated at the right hand of God. Set your minds on things above, not on earthly things'* (Colossians 3:1–2). Suppose you saw a rich celebrity, well known for their mansion and vast wealth, sitting at a London tube station with a piece of cardboard and a mangy dog begging for a few extra pence. You'd think they were crazy. It's just as crazy to run after the things the pagans do when we have an inheritance in heaven beyond imagining.

So many of us haven't got the balance between time and money right because we live under the perpetual illusion that if we just worked a little harder, earned a little more, bought a few more things, went on better holidays – then we would be happy. For others the issue is one of security. We think that with a bit more income, a better pension, a smaller mortgage, our future can be secure. To someone who thought like that, God said: *'You fool! This very night your life will be demanded from you'* (Luke 12:20; see also Matthew 6:19–20).

Christians can be the busiest people of all because we want it all. We have a foot in both camps. We have better things to do – kingdom things, gospel things. But we also want the trappings of this world. We work hard for the treasure of heaven.

But we also work hard for the treasure of earth. So we're running around twice as much as the pagans. 'Our churches do not dispense with the worship of the Lord,' comments Jim Wallis (1981). 'They simply include the worship of other gods. We want God's life, but we want the good life too.'

Buying time

One way to get more time is to buy it! Holidays, cars, possessions, a better house are all 'false satisfiers'. And they all require money. The 'true satisfiers' are relationships, friendships, purpose, service and, above all, God himself. They all require time. Why work more than nine to five? Why do you need promotion? Why do both partners need jobs? To afford to live. But to live what? To live a standard of living that you have presumed you need or want or should have? It is a life full of false satisfiers. We work our guts out to be well-off without ever really asking what it means to be 'well-off'.

I know several people who have decided to work four days a week and give a day to relationships and ministry. It's not an option open to everyone, but it may be for you. Malcolm is a new convert who works in our local supermarket. Even though he earns only £5 an hour, he's decided to work four days a week instead of five so he has more time for people in the church. You may wonder how you could live on a fifth less than you're currently earning – going, say, from £25,000 to £20,000. But plenty of people do live on £20,000, £15,000 or less. In fact you probably did in the past. It's a question of getting rid of some of those false satisfiers. If you *can't* live on a smaller salary, then maybe you're enslaved. In one Mennonite church in Indiana, USA, every member is a part of a small group in which they pray and study Scripture together. But, says Tom Sine, 'twice a year they do something that terrifies American Evangelicals when I tell them about it. Twice a year they bring their timetables and their budgets to the group. They ask everyone in their group to hold them mutually accountable for how they plan to use their time and money in the next six months in their struggle to put God's purposes first' (Sine, 1999).

Paul Tripp sometimes says to groups of men: 'Some of you are not spending enough time with your children. You need to ask for a demotion and move to a smaller house.' On one occasion a man came up to him afterwards. He had heard Paul say something similar two years before. 'I was so mad at you,' he confessed. 'If I'd been able to talk to you afterwards, there'd have been trouble!' But he went on to explain how the words had haunted him, and one month later he had gone to talk to his boss about his role. 'But we've fast-tracked you as quick as we can,' his boss said. 'No, you misunderstand,' the man explained, 'I want a demotion so I can spend more time with my family.' The boss was astonished. Even when he explained it would mean a drop in salary, the man was determined. Finally the boss said: 'I've never heard of someone doing this before and I don't think I will again.' The family sold their dream house for a smaller one and exchanged their new cars for old ones. 'In the two years since,' the man explained to Paul, 'my children have never once complained about losing the big house or new cars, but they've often thanked me for being more involved in their lives.' Finally he pointed his finger at Paul: 'You keep on telling people to ask for demotion!'

Bob Holman was Professor of Social Policy at Bath University until he made the decision to 'downsize'. He became a community worker in a socially deprived area of Glasgow. 'My motivation was complex,' he told *The Guardian* newspaper. 'I was not much of a professor. I felt guilty about earning a large salary while lecturing on poverty. But the most important reason related to my understanding of Christianity. In Jesus Christ, I saw one who was alongside the powerless not the powerful' (Holman, 2003). His main reflection 25 years on, however, is how much he's gained. 'I have benefited by being downwardly mobile. As an academic, I had colleagues whom I saw at work and social gatherings. But the relationships tended to be shallow and short-lived as one of us moved on to a higher position. Within deprived areas, I have been closer to people because we spend much more time with each other in the neighbourhood where we live. We have bonded over years of common practices. I have enjoyed deep relationships that have given me love, support and companionship.'

Tony Payne (2002) imagines what genuinely Christian television might be like.

> I would particularly look forward to the new versions of *Changing Rooms* and *Better Homes*. They would become five-minute programmes called *Perfectly Adequate Homes and Gardens*. Each week, a former bricklayer or plumber would take us on a tour of a bog-standard family home, and say, 'As you can see, the Wilson family home has plenty of potential. There's lots we could do with this one. However, it does the job pretty well. It's warm and dry and comfortable. No obvious structural problems. We're going to encourage the Wilsons to be content and leave it as it is.' Cut to closing credits.

'That such a programme seems absurd,' he comments, 'is testimony to the extent to which we have all accepted the premise of *Ground Force* and all the lifestyle programmes of that genre – namely that of course we all want our homes and gardens to be better, our wealth wealthier, our health healthier, and our sex sexier.' Each year we spend £12.5 billion on

DIY, £2.4 billion of it over the Easter weekend. We still worship at Easter, but our god has changed.

The first chapter of Haggai is about time management. The people say: *'The time has not yet come for the LORD's house to be built'* (verse 2). But Haggai says: *'Is it a time for you yourselves to be living in your panelled houses, while this house remains a ruin?'* (verse 4). While my house remains a ruin, says God, *'each of you is busy with his own house'* (verse 9). They were a DIY makeover generation just like ours. What mattered to them were their panelled houses. They were busy people: busy at work increasing their incomes; busy at home improving their houses. Many of us are just the same. So listen to God's word to them: *'You have planted much, but have harvested little. You eat, but never have enough. You drink, but never have your fill. You put on clothes, but are not warm. You earn wages, only to put them in a purse with holes in it'* (verse 6). All their effort brings no reward. They are not satisfied. The LORD says he blew away their harvest and sent drought on their fields. *'You expected much,'* he says, *'but see, it turned out to be little'* (verse 9). They are busy with earthly treasure and God in his mercy will not let them be satisfied with earthly treasure. There are many people who can't rest because they are running after something they can't catch. They're chasing satisfaction and fulfilment, but in the wrong direction. The faster they run, the further away they are from their goal.

Riches have a habit of creating new wants rather than satisfying old ones. God will not let us be satisfied with anything less than himself.

'I'm busy because I need the money' is a lie. The truth is that God alone is my joy.

'I'm busy because I need the money' is a lie. The truth is that God alone is my joy.

A pure heart – a meditation on Psalm 73

Surely God is good to Israel,
to those who are pure in heart.
² But as for me, my feet had almost slipped;
I had nearly lost my foothold.
³ For I envied the arrogant
when I saw the prosperity of the wicked.
⁴ They have no struggles;
their bodies are healthy and strong.
⁵ They are free from the burdens common to man;
they are not plagued by human ills.
⁶ Therefore pride is their necklace;
they clothe themselves with violence.
⁷ From their callous hearts comes iniquity;
the evil conceits of their minds know no limits.
⁸ They scoff, and speak with malice;
in their arrogance they threaten oppression.
⁹ Their mouths lay claim to heaven,
and their tongues take possession of the earth.
¹⁰ Therefore their people turn to them
and drink up waters in abundance.
¹¹ They say, 'How can God know?
Does the Most High have knowledge?'
¹² This is what the wicked are like –
always carefree, they increase in wealth.

This is a Psalm about what it means to be pure in heart. God is good to the pure in heart (verse 1). But, says the Psalmist, he seems to be just as good to the wicked. He sees greedy people who disregard God and they seem to get on in life. How do cowboy builders, corporate climbers, tax evaders and benefit cheats make you feel? How do you feel about those who live for wealth and possessions? Envious, frustrated, guilty?

> [13] *Surely in vain have I kept my heart pure;*
> *in vain have I washed my hands in innocence.*
> [14] *All day long I have been plagued;*
> *I have been punished every morning.*

A pure heart set on God and living for him seems to be a waste of time. It just brings a day-full of troubles. Purity of heart is hard work when the world around us is heading in the opposite direction. This is life in the real world. Are you tempted to worship God in church and worship mammon at the shopping centre? Are you tempted to live for God on Sundays and live for promotion on Mondays?

> [15] *If I had said, 'I will speak thus,'*
> *I would have betrayed your children.*
> [16] *When I tried to understand all this,*
> *it was oppressive to me*
> [17] *till I entered the sanctuary of God;*
> *then I understood their final destiny.*
> [18] *Surely you place them on slippery ground;*
> *you cast them down to ruin.*
> [19] *How suddenly are they destroyed,*
> *completely swept away by terrors!*
> [20] *As a dream when one awakes,*
> *so when you arise, O Lord,*
> *you will despise them as fantasies.*
> [21] *When my heart was grieved*
> *and my spirit embittered,*
> [22] *I was senseless and ignorant;*
> *I was a brute beast before you.*

In the presence of God the Psalmist realizes the final
destiny of the wicked. What is going on around him is not the
last word. The wicked do prosper now, but their success is
temporary because God's judgment is coming. Think of
prosperous or powerful people who have fallen from power.
They are a sign of what is coming. Create a wish list of things
you would like to own. How valuable will they be to you in
ten years time, in fifty years time, in eternity? The wealth and
prestige we covet so much is temporary and fragile (Luke
12:16–21).

> *²³ Yet I am always with you;*
> *you hold me by my right hand.*
> *²⁴ You guide me with your counsel,*
> *and afterwards you will take me into glory.*
> *²⁵ Whom have I in heaven but you?*
> *And earth has nothing I desire besides you.*
> *²⁶ My flesh and my heart may fail,*
> *but God is the strength of my heart*
> *and my portion for ever.*

Our future is glory (verse 24). We will enjoy the presence
of God without pain or tears. The future for the pure in heart
is nothing less than God himself. He is our portion (verse 26).
'Blessed are the pure in heart,' says Jesus, *'for they will see God'*
(Matthew 5:8). In verse 9 the wicked lay claim to heaven and
take possession of the earth. They end up with terror and
destruction. But we can say: *'Whom have I in heaven but you?*
And earth has nothing I desire besides you' (verse 25). Nothing can
compare with knowing the glorious, holy, beautiful, perfect,
loving God. There is no greater good, no greater blessing, no
greater reward than God himself. What do you desire? How
does it compare with knowing God?

[27] Those who are far from you will perish;
you destroy all who are unfaithful to you.
[28] But as for me, it is good to be near God.
I have made the Sovereign LORD my refuge;
I will tell of all your deeds.

In verse 2 the Psalmist says: *'But as for me . . .'* He is about to slip because he envies the wealth of the wicked. In verse 28 he says it again. But now he doesn't want to be like the wealthy. He's discovered something much better: to be near God. That's the truly good thing in life. The coming Judge provides himself as a refuge. He takes his judgment on himself in our place so that we can enjoy him for ever. The psalm doesn't end by telling us to do good deeds. It ends by telling of God's saving deeds.

To know my Jesus crucified,
by far excels all things beside;
all earthly goods we count but loss
and triumph in our Saviour's cross.

Knowledge of all terrestrial things
never our souls true pleasure brings;
no peace, but in the Son of God;
no joy, but through his pardoning blood.

O could I know and love him more
and all his wondrous grace explore,
I would not envy man's esteem,
but part with all and follow him.

Richard Burnham (1749–1810)

12. I'M BUSY BECAUSE I WANT TO MAKE THE MOST OF LIFE – *THE LIBERATING HOPE OF GOD*

Working hard and playing hard

Why are we busy? Because there's so much to do! There's so much to learn; there are so many places to visit and so many things to see. The modern world contains so many possibilities, at least for those in wealthy nations. No wonder we're busy. There's a whole world out there for us to experience. Leisure has become hard work. We have become experience junkies. For some people a holiday is a chance to lie on the beach, read a book, stroll in the country. But for other people it's a chance to see the sites, take the photos, visit the museum, 'do' London. We want to do everything while we have the chance. We want to 'live life to the max'.

We project this approach on our children. My wife is a teacher. She frequently has parents of primary age children asking for more homework. Children are under pressure to do well in exams from as early as seven. They need to do well at school if they're to get good grades, if they're to go to a good university, if they're to get a good job, if they're to get on in their careers, if they're to earn enough to send their children to good schools, if *they're* to do well at school . . . and so it goes on. And even when they come home children can't 'just play'. We ferry them from one activity to another so they can experience life to the full, so they can realize their potential. And then parents complain that they're busy running a taxi service for their children. A mother told a friend of mine recently that she was worried her son doesn't do that much – just scouts, diving and music lessons. My friend suggested that this might be more than enough! But the mother said that most of his friends were doing far more. A recent cartoon showed two little girls waiting for the school bus clutching their personal organizers: 'Okay, I'll move ballet back an hour, reschedule gymnastics and cancel piano . . . You shift your violin lessons to Thursday and skip soccer practice . . . That gives us from 3.15 to 3.45 on Wednesday the 16th to play' (cited in Honoré, 2004).

Our grandparents lived fairly defined lives. If you were born working class you would probably die working class. If you were born in Manchester you would probably die in Manchester. You would stay in one profession most of your life, quite possibly in one job. Indeed it was probably a similar job to your father's. But all that has changed. Universal education and rising prosperity have given us more choices than ever. We may not yet live in a classless society, but more careers than ever are open to young people. Progressing up the corporate ladder is not out of the question. The common assumption is that everyone has the right, maybe even the duty, to 'realize their potential' and 'go as far as they can'. 'It's your life,' we're told, 'you've got to make the most of it.' Bettering yourself, finding your identity, defining and redefining your place in the world – these are the duties of our modern age. And so we are busy.

In his influential book, *New Rules: Searching for Self-Fulfilment in a World Turned Upside-Down,* Daniel Yankelovich (1982) describes a new ethic – 'the duty to self ethic' – which is replacing the old ethic of self-denial, duty to others and deferred gratification. Now self-fulfilment is the priority, even if it overrides loyalties to marriage and community. Yankelovich tells many stories to illustrate this. Cynthia Muller, for example, initially enjoyed staying at home with her first child. But she worried about being 'just a housewife'. After three years she returned to work 'mainly for my self-fulfilment, but also because the money came in handy'. Cynthia and her husband David used the extra income to buy a larger house. But now they feel trapped. Now they 'need' Cynthia's salary to keep up the mortgage payments. They take it in turns caring for their daughter with the result that they live separate lives – more business partners than married couple. The search for self-fulfilment through work and through possessions has left them over-busy. Professor James Davison Hunter (1987) used some of Yankelovich's research methods and found that evangelical students were *more* committed to self-fulfilment than the general population.

Finite people in a finite world

There was something different about the seventh day of creation. And it wasn't just that God rested. Every other day in the story of creation ends with the words: *'And there was evening, and there was morning – the first day'* (Genesis 1:5, etc.). But not the seventh day. This is a day without end. God didn't go back to work the next week. Now that the work of creation is complete, an eternity of rest has begun.

In the biblical worldview, a person's life is a small drama played out in the divine–human cosmic drama. With the rise of humanism the focus has shifted to a purely human drama.

God has disappeared from the picture – in practical terms, at least. Life is no longer a brief interval in eternity. People's horizons are entirely focused on this world. Goals have to be fulfilled in this lifetime and so each day time must be used intensively. We have secularized time. It is no longer time in eternity. It's just time. Christians are not immune. I was once involved in planning a missions conference. I wanted to focus on eschatology – the Christian understanding of the future – but was told missions people weren't interested in eschatology. Eschatology and eternity aren't 'useful'. It's the immediate that counts. This life is all we are interested in.

The BBC ran a survey to find out what people wanted to do before they died. Number 1 was to swim with a dolphin. Number 18 was to see the earth from space. A lot of people are going to die disappointed! Whether they dream of seeing the earth from space, having a happy marriage, starting their own business or living in the country, most people are not going to achieve their dreams. Part of the pathos of the TV comedy series *The Office* is the fear we all have of waking up one day and finding that our dreams have been reduced to hitting a monthly sales target.

One of the reasons people today are so busy is that they must do everything in one lifetime. Samuel Johnson had 'The Night Cometh' inscribed on his watch. Sir Walter Scott had it inscribed on his sundial. The words are taken from John 9:4: *'Night is coming, when no-one can work.'* But Johnson and Scott didn't understand the words the way Jesus intended. Jesus, the Light of the World, was speaking of his departure. For Johnson and Scott it was a reminder of mortality. They had to achieve fame in this life before it was over.

Everything must be compressed into one lifetime. As an advert for the X-Box says: 'Life is short. Play more.' Leisure is hard work because we are trying to fit an eternity of experiences into one, short lifespan. This is why people have mid-life crises. It's the moment when they realize time is running out. They embark on a desperate attempt to do the things they think they ought to have done when they were young (on mid-life, see Tripp, 2004). Or else people are trying to prolong their lives. We try to stay young, look young, feel young. We go to the gym, have a makeover, even have cosmetic surgery. To the busyness of our lives we add the time-consuming task of staying young.

The truth: an eternal future

The Roman philosopher Seneca observed: 'We are always complaining that our days are few, and at the same time acting as if they would never end.' But Christians can act as if our days will never end! We don't have to squeeze everything into one lifetime. It may be that in eternity we will get the chance to do hundreds of things we missed out in this life. Maybe we

> *We don't have to squeeze everything into one lifetime.*

will get to fly among the stars and see the earth from space. I would love to spend time gardening, but I'm happy to defer this pleasure to the new creation so I can give my time to other things in this life. And if I don't get to do much gardening in heaven, I know I won't feel that as regret or loss!

We're often told that today is the first day of the rest of your life. It's an aphorism designed to motivate us to start straight away on some new life-changing venture. We need to get on with life. But, as comedian Bill Bailey points out in *Part Troll*, it's also true that '*the day after tomorrow* is the first day of the rest of your life – that way you've always got a couple of days in hand . . . just to muck about.'

Sinful people in a sinful world

In his book *Second Choice*, Viv Thomas (2000) says: 'In our ideal world we choose our job, spouse, city, entertainment, company, community and religion at leisure with freedom . . . In the real world things do not work that smoothly. Even if we have the opportunity to employ our power of choice, the first choice tends to go wrong.' We have to learn to live within our second-choice world. Some people are busy because they are still pursuing the mirage of their first-choice world.

We are sinful people living in a sinful world. We mess up. Other people mess up. Sickness, suffering, death continue to be a reality. This world has not yet been redeemed. After all, argues Paul, *'hope that is seen is no hope at all. Who hopes for what he already has? But if we hope for what we do not yet have, we wait for it patiently'* (Romans 8:24–25). In the New Testament the corollaries of hope are patience and long-suffering. But patience and long-suffering are not common characteristics in our culture. We expect good health as a norm. We call for public enquiries because we think every disaster can be avoided. Christians are not so very different. We expect God to keep us healthy and safe. So when trouble comes – as Jesus promises it will (John 16:33) – we not only struggle to cope with the problem, we can't make sense of what God is doing.

One day this world will share the glory of Christ's resurrection. Everything will be made new. *'There will be no more death or mourning or crying or pain.'* The old order of things will pass away (Revelation 21:4). But that day has not yet arrived. The resurrection is the sign of what is to come. In the meantime the cross is the sign of history. This is the world we live in: a world that murders its Creator; a god-forsaken world of sin, suffering and death. The pattern of discipleship is the pattern of suffering followed by glory – the pattern of the cross and the resurrection modelled by Jesus

(1 Peter 1:11). Peter tells us to *'rejoice that you participate in the suffering of Christ, so that you may be overjoyed when his glory is revealed'* (1 Peter 4:13). We have resurrection power now, but so that we might live the life of the cross. It is power to be weak (2 Corinthians 4:7–12; Philippians 3:10–11). Our resurrection life is a hidden life, revealed in conformity with Christ and his cross (Colossians 3:1–4). John White (1992) observes: 'From all over the Western world, where Christians enjoy liberty and prosperity, I receive letters requesting seminars on eliminating stress. The letters trouble me. They stand in contrast to letters from some Third-World countries where Christians are persecuted and thus under tremendous stress. From these countries come letters requesting instruction on faithfulness and on the cost of discipleship.' White's reflection on this phenomenon is that Third-World Christians take stress for granted as part of normal Christian living.

One mother of three said to me: 'I found it so helpful to realize that this was the way my life was.' That's biblical realism and it's liberating. She didn't have to strive to live the perfect life portrayed in the glossy magazines. I remember when our younger child was about five. I felt strange, but couldn't figure out why. After a few days I finally twigged what it was: I didn't feel tired. For eight or so years, while our daughters were young, we had broken nights interspersed by energy-sapping days of childcare. Mind-numbing tiredness had become so normal that *not* feeling tired was weird. That's the way it is. Get used to it. And don't worry about it. Don't worry about missing out. Some of your friends may be out late partying, jetting round the world, climbing the corporate ladder. But this is the life God has given you – and he is always wise and always good.

Jonathan is a Christian worker who has complained of feeling tired and overworked ever since I've known him. I tried working through his priorities with him, but it made no difference. He recently took a three-month sabbatical because he was worn out. At the end, he was still complaining about feeling tired. Now he wants to 'operate in his gifting'. And funnily enough his gifting doesn't include administration and paperwork. He only wants to do what he enjoys. Anything else makes him weary. But that's the way life is! Sometimes work is energizing and exciting. But everyone has irksome responsibilities that make them feel weary. Indeed, for most people in the world, their work is mainly drudgery. It's arrogant and selfish to suppose you have a right to do only what energizes you when most people spend their lives on factory production lines or bent over in fields. We can't design perfect working lives because we don't yet live a perfect world. Jonathan doesn't need another sabbatical or a new job. He needs to learn self-control and self-denial. Paul talks about spiritual gifts so we value the diversity in the church. He doesn't tell individual Christians to identify their gifting and stick to it. He tells Christians to be servants, looking to the interests of others and modelling ourselves on the self-giving of the cross.

The truth: a better future

When Jesus invited the weary to come and find 'rest' (Matthew 11:28–30), his invitation didn't come out of the blue. It was full of Old Testament resonance. God redeemed the people of Israel that they might enjoy rest from their enemies in the land of blessing – a rest linked with his presence with his people (Exodus 33:14; Deuteronomy 12:8–11). Sabbath and temple are parallel notions. The temple was a space within space that was particularly God's. And Sabbath was a time within time that was particularly God's. All space and all time belong to God and are indwelt by God, but the temple and

Sabbath were 'holy' to God so that in them people might 'remember' God. In the new Jerusalem, however, there will be no temple because God is present with his people in an unmediated form. In the same way Sabbath points to our participation in the eternal rest of God.

To some extent Israel found rest under Joshua's leadership (Joshua 21:44). But Joshua couldn't give the people complete or lasting rest (Hebrews 4:8–10). When the people turned from God, God left the Canaanites in the land as thorns in their sides (Judges 2:1–3). The land would no longer be a place of rest. David gave the people rest from their enemies for a time (2 Samuel 7:1), but it was short-lived. Ultimately God's people were overrun by their enemies and went into exile. The promise of rest became associated with the reign of David's descendant (2 Samuel 7:10–11; 1 Chronicles 22:9). Rest was forfeited by Israel's disobedience (Lamentations 1:3; Micah 2:10), but the prophets promised that God's coming King would again bring rest (Isaiah 11:10). Jesus' promise that the weary *'will find rest for your souls'* (Matthew 11:29) is a quotation from the prophet Jeremiah (6:16). In Hebrews 4 we are told the rest of God is something we can enter by faith in the gospel (verses 1–4). The failure of Israel to enter God's rest means the promise of rest still stands for us (verses 5–11).

So the invitation to find rest in Jesus is not a statement of individual piety. It is an 'exodus' statement. It is the promise of liberation – liberation *from* the enemies of sin, religious law and death, and liberation *into* God's reign of blessing and rest. Jesus' invitation to rest is followed by conflict with the Pharisees over the Sabbath (Matthew 12:1–21). The law of Moses brought mercy and freedom in contrast to Pharaoh's oppressive rule, but the Pharisees had made the law itself oppressive. But now the Lord of the Sabbath is here bringing the liberation to which the law pointed. The Sabbath day healings of Jesus illustrate his Sabbath reign. The promised King is bringing salvation and freedom.

You may think you're missing out in life because you're still single or because you're in a dead-end job or you flunked your exams or messed up your marriage or you're not very fit or you can't afford your dream home in the country. But a better world is coming for the children of God. You don't need to rush around having every experience going. You don't need to 'realize your potential'. You just need to glorify God and enjoy him for ever. You don't need to give yourself a breakdown trying to create a perfect life. Christ has already given himself to create a perfect life. Your role is to wait patiently. What should we do about our busyness? We should wait. Wait for the eternal rest of God. *'Then I heard a voice from heaven say, "Write: Blessed are the dead who die in the Lord from now on." "Yes," says the Spirit, "they will rest from their labour, for their deeds will follow them"'* (Revelation 14:13).

✠

A wise heart – a meditation on Psalm 90

According to Psalm 90 the normal life of a person is 'three score years and ten' – seventy years (verse 10). Does that seem a long way off to you, or are you already in extra time? Or maybe you've recently passed the half-way mark and are having a bit of mid-life crisis. You're questioning your achievements, pondering your missed opportunities, mourning the lives you didn't live. People want to be remembered. We want significance and permanence.

A Prayer of Moses, the man of God
Lord, you have been our dwelling place in all generations.
² Before the mountains were brought forth,

or ever you had formed the earth and the world,
from everlasting to everlasting you are God (ESV).

Generations of God's people had lived in tents with no permanent resting place, but they have found a permanent dwelling place in God himself. The people of no fixed abode could give God as their address. Think what it's like to stand on a mountain – to have a solid mass of rock beneath you, something that has been around for thousands of years. Mountains are proverbial for being immovable and permanent. But God precedes them for he has no beginning and no end.

3 You return man to dust
and say, 'Return, O children of man!'
4 For a thousand years in your sight
are but as yesterday when it is past,
or as a watch in the night.
5 You sweep them away as with a flood; they are like a dream,
like grass that is renewed in the morning:
6 in the morning it flourishes and is renewed;
in the evening it fades and withers (ESV).

Compared to God we are temporary and fragile. Verse 3 is a reference to Genesis 3:19: we are of the dust and to dust God returns us. An American friend told me his church was 'very old – 130 years'. As a Brit, I laughed because for us 130 years is recent. Some historian friends showed our family round Hampton Court Palace. They kept talking about 'the new bit' which is 200 years old and 'the old bit' which is 500 years old. Do the maths: 500 years is just a morning for God! Think over all that happened in human history in the last millennium, the empires and movements that came and went. It all passed in a moment for the God of eternity. Moses gives us three pictures which show how fragile and transitory we are:

- Debris in a flood: recall TV images of floods sweeping all before them.
- A forgotten dream: have you woken in the middle of a dream and found that you couldn't remember it?
- Withered grass: pick a flower in the morning, put it on a sunny window sill and look at it again in the evening.

Think about your dreams of being someone special, of achieving something, of making the most of life. How do they look in the eyes of the eternal God? Psalm 39:6 says: *'all our busy rushing ends in nothing'* (NLT). We're busy doing nothing. Praise God because he is a permanent dwelling place for his fragile people.

> [7] *For we are brought to an end by your anger;*
> *by your wrath we are dismayed.*
> [8] *You have set our iniquities before you,*
> *our secret sins in the light of your presence.*
> [9] *For all our days pass away under your wrath;*
> *we bring our years to an end like a sigh.*
> [10] *The years of our life are seventy,*
> *or even by reason of strength eighty;*
> *yet their span is but toil and trouble;*
> *they are soon gone, and we fly away* (ESV).

Our days are short *not* because we were made that way. Our days are short because of God's judgment. Our problem is not that we are creatures, but that we are sinners. Because of God's anger we experience life as *'toil and trouble'* and life ends in death.

¹¹ Who considers the power of your anger,
and your wrath according to the fear of you?
¹² So teach us to number our days
that we may get a heart of wisdom (ESV).

The request of the Psalm is this: *'teach us to number our days that we may get a heart of wisdom'*. It's not an exercise in numeracy or time management. It's not about *how many* days we have left. It's about remembering *why* we have a limited number. It's about realizing the power of God's anger for this is what cuts short our days (verse 11). The *'man of God'* (verse 1) measures time by living as someone who is going to die under God's wrath. *'A heart of wisdom'* in verse 12 is not about knowledge or skill. Wisdom is to acknowledge our true relationship to God as our Creator and Judge. A wise heart is a humble heart that fears God.

¹³ Return, O Lord! How long?
Have pity on your servants!
¹⁴ Satisfy us in the morning with your steadfast love,
that we may rejoice and be glad all our days.
¹⁵ Make us glad for as many days as you have afflicted us,
and for as many years as we have seen evil.
¹⁶ Let your work be shown to your servants,
and your glorious power to their children (ESV).

Since we die under God's wrath, we number our days by calling on God for mercy. In verse 3 God returns man to dust: he moves man from life to death, from significance to insignificance. Now Moses prays for God to return: to reverse his actions so that he moves man from death to life, from insignificance to significance. We don't find life and significance because of any merit of our own. Our actions lead to death (verses 7–11). We find life and significance through God's pity (verse 13) and steadfast love (verse 14). Use the words of verses 13–16 to pray to God for mercy.

> *¹⁷ Let the favour of the Lord our God be upon us,*
> *and establish the work of our hands upon us;*
> *yes, establish the work of our hands!* (ESV).

This is a surprising end to the Psalm. We don't expect a meditation on the transitoriness of human beings and human achievement to end with a prayer to establish the work of our hands. But through God's mercy and in partnership with God we can achieve something of significance. We can do work that counts for all eternity. The message of this Psalm is that our impermanence is not the result of creation, but of the fall. We were not made to be small, transitory and insignificant – that was the result of our sin. We were made to be significant, to live forever, to be partners with God. And through the mercy of God, we can again be partners with God working for what will last.

In Genesis 11 the people of the world gather to build a tower up to the heavens. They say: *'we may make a name for ourselves'* (Genesis 11:4). But God thwarts their plans, which come to nothing. In Genesis 12 God promises Abraham a people and a land. He says: *'I will make your name great'* (Genesis 12:2). The way to greatness is to be part of God's saving purposes. The promise to Abraham is the beginning of a story. Moses now leads God's people. Psalm 90 may well be a prayer for God to end Israel's slavery in Egypt (reread it with that mind and see what you think). It's the story that comes to a climax with the death and resurrection of Jesus. And we can be characters in the story. Jesus gave us authority to makes disciples of all nations (Matthew 28:18–20). The

story of Abraham to Moses to Jesus to the ends of the earth
– this is the thing of significance in human history. And we
find significance as we play our part in this story. Jesus said:
'*whoever wants to save his life will lose it, but whoever loses his life
for me and for the gospel will save it*' (Mark 8:35). Think about
how you spend your time. What are you doing that will end
up like debris swept away by a flood, like a forgotten dream,
like withered grass? What are you doing that will last for all
eternity? Ask God to establish the work of your hands.

CONCLUSION: FINDING REST IN THE MIDST OF BUSYNESS

We have seen six lies that can make us over-busy. We are driven to do too much by the desire to prove ourselves, or meet other people's expectations, or control our lives, or hide from our problems, or find satisfaction in possessions, or make the most of this life. These things make us do too much.

But it's also important to realize that neither doing more nor doing less is really the answer. We sometimes think if we worked a little harder then we could get on top of the problem. Or we think that cutting back what we do will make the problem go away. But neither doing more nor doing less will resolve the pressures created when we don't trust God. If I'm busy because I feel the pressure to prove myself, neither doing more nor doing less will help. Doing more won't help because we can never do enough to justify ourselves. And doing less won't help because it won't address the underlying desire for justification. Only the truth sets us free. The answer is neither doing more nor doing less. The answer is faith in God.

Christians should be busy people. We should be *'poured out'* (Philippians 2:17). We give our lives to Christ and no longer claim our time as our own. We work *'night and day, labouring and toiling'* (2 Thessalonians 3:8). Our faith produces work, our love prompts labour and our hope inspires endurance (1 Thessalonians 1:3). We work as those whose deeds will follow them into eternity (Revelation 14:13).

But we can find rest *in* our busyness and joy in our labour. The yoke that Jesus gives is easy and his burden is light (Matthew 11:30). We are busy, but we can be free from the drivenness that makes busyness a burden. I can rest in the midst of busyness because:

- trusting God to be my Saviour sets me free from the pressure to prove myself
- trusting God to be my Master sets me free from the weight of other people's expectations
- trusting God to be my Provider sets me free from the fear that things will get out of control
- trusting God to be my Refuge sets me free from the compulsion to hide behind my busyness
- trusting God to be my Joy sets me free from the vain pursuit of satisfaction in possessions
- trusting God to be my Hope sets me free from the frantic need to make the most of this life.

In each case we can find rest in our busyness by believing the truth about God. Busyness is all about our response to God. The answer to our busyness must be theological. I don't mean theological in the sense of academic. Theology is what we think about God. And our busyness turns on how we view God.

'The joy of the LORD is your strength' (Nehemiah 8:10). It is a truth borne out in my own experience and in my observations of other people. More often than not, those who complain about their busyness are those who are not finding joy in God. And those who rejoice in God as their Saviour, Master, Provider, Refuge, Joy and Hope do not find their busyness a burden.

> *More often than not, those who complain about their busyness are those who are not finding joy in God. And those who rejoice in God as their Saviour, Master, Provider, Refuge, Joy and Hope do not find their busyness a burden.*

There's an annual 'take your daughter to work day'. The aim is for girls to experience the world of work and break down prejudices about women's roles. How would you feel if your daughter or any other family member had spent the day with you yesterday? Would they have been impressed with the way you spend your time? What about a 'take your God to work day'? That's how Paul suggests we should view our work. We serve not just when others see us, but because *'the Lord will reward everyone for whatever good he does'* (Ephesians 6:7–8). Instead of measuring our lives in terms of tasks done and left undone, we should evaluate them in terms of time well spent or not well spent. When you put out the light at night why not pray, 'Father God, you've been with me all day. Have I spent my time well today?'

Taking God with you into the busyness of life means:

- resting on God our Saviour when we feel the need to prove ourselves
- serving God our Master when we worry about other people's expectations

- trusting God our Provider when we worry about things getting out of control
- making God our Refuge when we want to escape from busyness or through busyness
- enjoying God our Joy when we feel the attraction of over-working for more money
- waiting for God our Hope when we feel we have to make the most of life now.

Jesus said: *'Come to me, all you who are weary and burdened, and I will give you rest. Take my yoke upon you and learn from me, for I am gentle and humble in heart, and you will find rest for your souls'* (Matthew 11:28–29).

NOTES

Start here

Banks, Robert. *The Tyranny of Time* (IVP, 1983), p. 12.

Chapter One: Slow down, I want to get off!

Friedman, Meyer. Cited in: James Gleick, *Faster* (Little, Brown & Co, 1999), p. 16.

Jones, Alexandra. *About Time for Change* (The Work Foundation, 2003), p. 6.

Greene, Mark. 'Not Managing Today?' (http://www.licc. org.uk/culture/not-managing-today, 2/7/2004).

Goodman, Ellen. Cited in: Ruth Valerio, *L is for Lifestyle* (IVP, 2004).

Ward, Laura. *Foolish Words* (Robson Books, 2003), p. 69.

Putnam, Robert D. *Bowling Alone: The Collapse and Revival of American Community* (Simon & Schuster, 2000), p. 134.

Tripp, Paul David. *Instruments in the Redeemer's Hands* (P&R, 2002), p. 165.

Banks, Robert. '*With respect to time*', in: *The Tyranny of Time* (IVP, 1983), p. 32.

Banks, Robert. *'The clock, not the steam engine'*, Lewis Mumford cited in: *The Tyranny of Time, op. cit.*, p. 97.

Hobsbawn, E. J. *Industry and Empire* (Pelican, 1969), pp. 85–86.

Honoré, Carl. *'Working parents dealing with emails'*, in: *In Praise of Slow* (Orion, 2004), p. 9.

Powers, Richard. *The Paris Review Book for Planes, Trains, Elevators and Waiting Rooms* (Picador, 2004).

Putnam, Robert D. *'Feel rushed'*, in: *Bowling Alone, op. cit.*, p. 189.

Chapter Two: Is busy bad?

Ryken, Leland. *Work and Leisure in Christian Perspective* (IVP, 1989), p. 64.

Luther, Martin. Cited in: McGrath, Alister, *Roots That Refresh: A Celebration of Reformation Spirituality* (Hodder & Stoughton, 1991), p. 141.

Latimer, Hugh. Cited in: McGrath, Alister, *Roots That Refresh, op. cit.*, p. 143.

Perkins, William. Ryken, Leland, Cited in: *Work and Leisure in Christian Perspective* (IVP, 1989), p. 95.

Carlyle, Thomas. *'Man was created to work'*, cited in: Hodgkinson, Tom, *How to be Idle* (Hamish Hamilton, 2004), p. 23.

Carlyle, Thomas. 'There is a perennial nobleness', *Past and Present* (1843). Cited in: Thomas, Keith (ed.), *The Oxford Book of Work* (OUP, 1999), pp. 112–113.

Best, Geoffrey. *Mid-Victorian Britain 1851–75* (Fontana, 1979), pp. 94–95.

Smiles, Samuel. Cited in: Golby, J. M. (ed.) *Culture and Society in Britain 1850–1890* (Oxford, 1986), pp. 107–109.

Dickens, Charles. Cited in: Thomas, Keith (ed.), *The Oxford Book of Work* (OUP, 1999), p. 115.

Russell, Bertrand. *'In praise of idleness'*
(http://www.threads.name/russell/idleness.html, 1932).
Payne, Tony. *'The Rags of Time'*, The Briefing, No. 178/179, p. 11
(http://www.matthiasmedia.com.au/briefing/webextra/
rags_of_time.html, 2001).
Hodgkinson, Tom. *How to be Idle* (Hamish Hamilton, 2004), pp. 40–41.
M'Cheyne, R. M. Cited in: Andrew Bonar, *Memoir and Remains of R. M. M'Cheyne* (Banner of Truth, 1966), p. 14.
Hodgkinson, Tom. *'Around 8,000 people took holidays'*, in: *How to be Idle* (Hamish Hamilton, 2004), p. 244.
Seerveld, Calvin. *Rainbows for the Fallen World* (Toronto Tuppence Press, 1980), p. 53.

Chapter Three: Use your time efficiently

Andrew, Dave. *'Time . . . and what to do with it'*, The Briefing, No. 284 (May 2002), p. 17 (http://www.matthiasmedia.com.au/
briefing/webextra/dec03_time.htm, 2002).
Darley, John M. and Batson, C. Daniel. *'From Jerusalem to Jericho: A Study of Situational and Dispositional Variables in Helping Behaviour'*, in: *Journal of Personality and Social Psychology* 27:1 (1973), pp. 100–108.
Swift, Jonathan. *Gulliver's Travels* (Penguin, 1726, 1967), pp. 70–71.
Payne, Tony. *'The Rags of Time,'* The Briefing, No. 178/179, p. 11
(http://www.matthiasmedia.com.au/briefing/webextra/
rags_of_time.html, 2001).

Chapter Four: Sort out your priorities

Banks, Robert. *The Tyranny of Time* (IVP, 1983), p. 218.
Cranfield, C. E. B. *Romans*, Vol. II, International Critical Commentary Series (T &T Clark, 1975), p. 762.

Sine, Tom & Sine, Christine. *Living on Purpose: Finding God's Best for Your Life* (Monarch, 2002).

Croft, Steve. *Transforming Communities: Re-Imagining the Church for the 21st Century* (DLT: 2002), pp. 176–177.

Chester, Tim. *Delighting in the Trinity* (Monarch, 2005), especially chapter 10.

Chapter Five: Glorify God all the time

Parmiter, John. Prior, David. Cited in: *'Connecting with God in the Fast Lane'* (http://www.licc.org.uk/articles/ article.php/id/122, 2005).

Card, Michael. *'Come to the Cradle'* (Myrrh Records, 1993).

Fee, Gordon. *1 and 2 Timothy, Titus,* NIBC (Paternoster, 1995), pp. 74–76.

Blocher, Henri. *In the Beginning* (IVP, 1984), p. 57.

Vickers, Tim. *'The "X Factor" is in the "Why?"',* *Workwise* No. 18 (Dec 2004), p. 4.

Greene, Mark. *'Slave New World'* (http://www.licc.org.uk/articles/article.php/id/1, 2005). See also Mark Greene, *Supporting Christians at Work* (Administry/LICC, 2001).

Chester, Tim. *'More than a Private Faith',* chapter 2 of *Good News to the Poor* (IVP, 2004).

Chapter Six: Getting to the heart of busyness

Sanders, J. Oswald. *Problems of Christian Discipleship* (CIM, 1958), p. 12.

Bunting, Madeline. *Willing Slaves: How the Overwork Culture Is Ruling Our Lives* (HarperCollins, 2004).

Chapter Seven: I'm busy because I need to prove myself

Ryken, Leland. *Work and Leisure in Christian Perspective* (IVP, 1989), pp. 69–71 and chapter 4.

McGrath, Alister. *Roots That Refresh: A Celebration of Reformation Spirituality* (Hodder & Stoughton, 1991), p. 145.

Banks, Robert. *The Tyranny of Time* (IVP, 1983), p. 126.

Baab, Lynne. *Sabbath Keeping: Finding Freedom in the Rhythms of Rest* (IVP, 2005), p. 96.

Shepherd, Beverley. *'Hurry Sickness: Diagnosis & Cure?'* (http://www.licc.org.uk/articles/article.php/id/121, 2003).

Bauman, Zygmunt. *Work, Consumption and the New Poor* (OUP, 1998), p. 34.

Peters, Tom and Handy, Charles. Cited in: Madeleine Bunting, *Willing Slaves: How the Overwork Culture is Ruling Our Lives* (Harper Collins, 2004), p. 113.

Peters, Tom. Cited in: Bunting, Madeleine, *Willing Slaves, op cit.*, p. 113.

Bunting, Madeleine. *'Why the harried senior executive'*, in: *Willing Slaves, op. cit.*, p. 114.

Bunting, Madeleine. *'A work ethic has evolved'*, in: *Willing Slaves, op. cit.*, p. xxiv.

Bunting, Madeleine. *'The cleverness of the fit'*, in: *Willing Slaves, op. cit.*, p. 169.

Milne, Bruce. *The Message of John* (IVP, 1993), p. 283.

Powlison, David. *'This man isn't noisy inside'*, in: Powlison, David. *Seeing With New Eyes: Counselling and the Human Condition through the Lens of Scripture* (P&R, 2003), pp. 75–76.

Powlison, David. *'Your biggest problem'*, in: Powlison, David. *Seeing With New Eyes, op. cit.*, p. 86.

Powlison, David. *'Are you quiet inside?'*: in: Powlison, David. *Seeing With New Eyes, op. cit.*, p. 76.

Chapter Eight: I'm busy because of other people's expectations

Banks, Robert. *The Tyranny of Time* (IVP, 1983), p. 68.
Welch, Edward T. *'Are you over-committed?'*, in: *When People are Big and God is Small* (P&R, 1997), p. 15.
Welch, Edward T. *'We exalt other people'*, in: *When People are Big and God is Small, op. cit.*, pp. 44–45.
Tate, Nahum (1652–1715) and Brady, Nicholas (1659–1726)
'Fear him, ye saints', from the hymn: 'Through all the changing scenes of life'.

Chapter Nine: I'm busy because otherwise things get out of control

Sherman, Doug and Hendricks, William. *Your Work Matters to God* (NavPress, 1987), p. 203.
Brueggemann, Walter. *Genesis*, IBC (Knox, 1982), p. 35.
Marmot, Michael. In: *Nice Work*, Radio Four (13 July 2004).
Wright, N. T. *Following Jesus: Biblical Reflections of Discipleship* (SPCK, 1994), pp. 56 and 58.
White, John. *The Golden Cow* (MMS, 1979), pp. 41–42.
Tripp, Paul David. *Instruments in the Redeemer's Hands* (P&R, 2002), pp. 250–255.
Sammis, John H. (1846–1919). 'Trust and obey', from the hymn: 'When we walk with the Lord'.
Banks, Robert. *The Tyranny of Time* (IVP, 1983), p. 183.

Chapter Ten: I'm busy because I prefer being under pressure

Henegar, Walter. 'Putting Off Procrastination', *The Journal of Biblical Counselling* 20:1 (Fall 2001), p. 41.

Covey, Stephen. *The Seven Habits of Highly Effective People* (Simon & Schuster, 1992), p. 152.

Chapter Eleven: I'm busy because I need the money

Schwartz, Barry. *The Paradox of Choice: Why More is Less* (Harper Collins, 2004).

Bunting, Madeleine. *Willing Slaves: How the Overwork Culture is Ruling Our Lives* (Harper Collins, 2004), p. 165.

Chartered Institute of Personnel and Development. *Working Time Regulations: Calling Time on Working Time?* (CIPD, 2000), p. 4.

Honoré, Carl. *In Praise of Slow* (Orion, 2004), p. 189.

Office for National Statistics. *Social Trends* 35 (2005), p. 59.

Bunting, Madeleine. 'If someone complains', in: *Willing Slaves, op. cit.*, p. 155.

Hodgkinson, Tom. *How to be Idle* (Hamish Hamilton, 2004), p. 26.

Bunting, Madeleine. 'Consumerism has become', in: *Willing Slaves, op. cit.*, pp. 155 and 157.

Taylor, Dr & Mrs Howard. *Hudson Taylor In Early Years: The Growth of a Soul* (CIM, 1911), p. 347.

Yancey, Philip. *Rumours of Another World* (Zondervan, 2003), p. 238.

Lewis, C. S. 'The Weight of Glory,' in: *Essay Collection and Other Short Pieces* (Harper Collins, 2000), p. 96.

Kasser, Tim. *The High Price of Materialism* (MIT Press, 2003).

Wallis, Jim. *The Call to Conversion* (Lion, 1981), p. 30.

Sine, Tom. *Mustard Seed Versus McWorld* (Monarch, 1999), pp. 288–289.

Holman, Bob. 'Down-Sizing Provides New Wealth', *The Guardian* (13 December 2003).

Payne, Tony. 'The Secret of Contentment', *The Briefing* No. 282 (March 2002), p. 7.

Burnham, Richard (1749–1810). 'To know my Jesus crucified', hymn.

Chapter Twelve: I'm busy because I want to make the most of life

Honoré, Carl. *In Praise of Slow* (Orion, 2004), p. 10.
Yankelovich, Daniel. *New Rules: Searching for Self-Fulfilment in a World Turned Upside Down* (Bantam, 1982), pp. 16–17.
Hunter, James Davison. *Evangelicalism: The Coming Generation* (Chicago, 1987).
Tripp, Paul David. *Lost in the Middle: Midlife and the Grace of God* (Shepherd Press, 2004).
Thomas, Viv. *Second Choice: Embracing Life As It Is* (Paternoster, 2000), p. 3.
White, John. *Greater Than Riches* (IVP, 1992), p. 77.